Sleeping Giants

A Wake-Up Guide for First Line

Leaders of All Organizations

Sleeping Giants

A Wake-Up Guide for First Line

Leaders of All Organizations

Tony Barth

Wiaan de Beer

NA

NorthAmerican

Business Press

Atlanta – Seattle – South Florida – Toronto

North American Business Press, Inc
　　Atlanta, Georgia
　　Seattle, Washington
　　South Florida
　　Toronto, Canada

Sleeping Giants: A Wake-Up Guide for First Line Leaders of All Organizations

ISBN: 9780985394936
© 2012 All Rights Reserved.

Along with trade books for various business disciplines, the North American Business Press also publishes a variety of academic-peer reviewed journals.

Library of Congress Control Number: 2012953731

Library of Congress
Cataloging in Publication Division
101 Independence Ave., SE
Washington, DC 20540-4320
Printed in theUnited States of America

First Edition

This guide is dedicated to

Maureen, my beloved wife – You've been my loving
confidante and greatest supporter. Thank you for personally
being my LEADER giant.

Table of Contents

Acknowledgements from Tony Barth

A very special acknowledgment goes to my co-author, Wiaan de Beer. Wiaan's wonderful creativity, his thought provoking and challenging perspectives, and his engaging persona made the writing of <u>Sleeping Giants</u> a joyous partnership.

Casita Lynn's cover art and 6 sectional art illustrations are fantastic. Her iconography captures all of our conceptual ideas succinctly. Very special thanks for her time, genius, and talent. I am also very grateful to have enjoyed a long career to date, both as an internal and external management consultant, working with all levels of management in international and domestic organizations. Organizations that I have worked with over several years include: AgroFresh, Agway Inc, Cabrini College, Campbell's Soup, Certis, Corn Products International, Delaware County Community College, Dupont Dow Elastomers, FMC Corporation, FriendsLifeCare, Health Partners, Lenox China and Crystal, Long and Foster Realtors, PCS Phosphate, Penn State University, Philips Lighting Company, Rohm and Haas Company, Sealed Air Corporation, Sipcam Agro USA, The Home Depot, University of Delaware, University of Phoenix, Weichert Realtors and Western Electric Inc.

<u>Sleeping Giants</u> was created out of a sincere desire to help capture, in practical terms and words, many successful actions and behaviors that have helped First Line Leaders in the above-mentioned organizations. I would like to thank and acknowledge the many, many First Line Leaders I have personally gained knowledge and experience from on-the-job or in classroom training sessions - where a great deal of learning, sharing and friendships occurred. The personal stories and experiences shared by First Line LEADER giants have always been inspirational to me from a continuous learning standpoint. I salute these First Line Leaders because they truly provide an invaluable leadership and managerial cadre that organizations cannot successfully survive without.

What People Are Saying

"I've worked with Tony for over 20 years. He was the first to truly recognize the critical role of First Line Leaders. Simply promoting chemical operators to "foremen" is the easy step. Transforming them to legitimate managers responsible to the company in meeting goals consistent with corporate/business objectives is the difficult part. Tony is the best I've seen in doing this. Some of his students have told me they now feel part of the management team and their job, for the first time, is meaningful and fun. Thank you for Sleeping Giants."

Tom Mains

Human Resource and Labor Relations Manager, Rohm and Haas Company

"To all First Line Leaders, you no longer have to wait 20 years for the experience. Read Sleeping Giants now, and make an impact on the quality and success of your organization today."

Dianne Carmody

Strategic Planning Manager, Advanced Materials Division, The Dow Chemical Company

"Indispensable" is a word that comes to mind when reading and applying concepts outlined in Sleeping Giants. This is not a one-time read; rather, it was written to be used and applied on-the-job. Knowing the experience of the authors, this is what they want you to do, so do it!"

Don Strauss

Assistant General Manager, Human Resource Development Center, Panasonic

"This is a definitive guide and a must-read for strengthening any organization's management bench strength! Full of informative case stories, useful practical assessment and resource tools, it is a valuable tool for improving management *and* operational performance."

Susan Warner, JD

Director of Corporate Human Resources, FMC Corporation

Global Executive Director of Training, Organizational Development & Effectiveness, Sealed Air Corporation

"Once again Tony has demonstrated in <u>Sleeping Giants</u> cultural sensitivity for a subject that has long been on the backburner in favor of the more exotic topic of executive leadership. First line leadership is still the fundamental backbone of running a successful business in any country. Tony is right on target."

Gerd Mueller, Ph.D.

Director of Unisys University, Latin American Region, Unisys Corporation

"Strategy quickly becomes irrelevant if an organization lacks the capability at the front lines to be able to translate and execute it effectively. <u>Sleeping Giants</u> helps to provide the education, practical guidance, and inspiration for this key level of management. Thank you on behalf of executives and First Line Leaders!"

Dave Gartenberg

General Manager, Customer Services and Support Human Resources, Microsoft Inc.

"Sleeping Giants will provide First Line Leaders with a much needed tool for success that can be immediately applied on-the-job, where it matters most."

Bruce Hoechner

President and CEO, Rogers Corporation

"Sergeants are First Line Leaders and Non-Commissioned Officers are considered to be the 'backbone of the Army'—they are the foundation of every Army unit. Having successfully applied <u>Sleeping Giants</u>' wisdom in both corporate and military organizations, I am convinced that <u>Sleeping Giants</u> will become the essential guide for developing First Line Leaders."

Colonel George Schwartz

Brigadier General and Combat Veteran, Army National Guard of the United States

"I have seen when organizations invest in their front lines they are transformed and improvements are realized without capital investment. Senior managers have often been left wondering, 'How did this happen?' In Sleeping Giants, Barth & de Beer simply, 'Get it!'"

Dave Spirk

Director of Management/Organization Development and Staffing, Corn Products International

"First Line Leaders, as discussed in Sleeping Giants, are as important in the academic realm of higher education, as they are in the corporate world."

Mary H. Harris, Ph.D

Department Chair, Business, Cabrini College

"Critical and timely! Seeking competitive advantage? By now you have gained expertise in 6 sigma, lean, supply chain, stage-gate and other operational improvement methodologies. So what's next? As Tony Barth argues, convincingly, First Line Leaders can become a significant competitive lever for your organization. Tony is right!"

Nance Dicciani, Ph.D.

President and CEO, Honeywell Specialty Materials, Honeywell International Inc.

"In a service driven economy, we must have front line leaders who understand that the customer is the engine that drives our success. Servant leadership, strong teams, and a common goal are key. With strong coaching and outstanding training, our associates and leaders felt respected and supported, which translated to team commitment and business success. Thank you for Sleeping Giants."

Erich Schulz

District Manager, The Home Depot

Introduction

If you are a: Front-Line Manager, Supervisor, Department Head, Foreman, Section Leader, Group Leader, Team Leader, Project Leader, Sergeant, Squad Leader, Teacher/Educator, Coordinator, or Senior Professional then you are a *First Line Leader.* You are your organization's first line of offense and defense.

So what do First Line Leaders typically do? They make short-term decisions that directly impact and guide the performance of team members or subordinates. For instance, a sergeant drills his squad ahead of deployment; a store department head coordinates shift schedules; and a teacher guides a student's daily work activity. First Line Leaders provide direction or coaching to non-supervisory personnel and typically provide performance assessment and recognition of team members.

You and your organization may not recognize, respect, and appreciate your significant role as a First Line Leader, and when your significance is not recognized, utilized, and reinforced -- you become a sleeping giant. It's time to ask the difficult question: Am I a sleeping giant?

Organizations tolerate sleeping giants because training and development of giants requires attention, effort and money. Has your organization under-trained and under-developed you? Is your organization being shortsighted about your potential to contribute? A "yes" answer to either question is the sound of being subdued and lulled to sleep. If this is the case, you and your organization are in trouble!

Sleeping giants -- THIS IS YOUR WAKE-UP CALL! Waking-up means there is a new awareness that you need to be both an effective manager and an effective leader. Do you know what "effective" truly means? Giants are looked up to because they stand out. But standing out for being an eyesore is vastly different to standing out for inspirational management and leadership.

First Line Leadership is a challenging management level to perform, because you are required to fulfill a vital linchpin role that ensures strategic and operational alignment with middle and top management. You are expected to support your larger organization's mission, vision, and key goals and initiatives. You provide daily operational support and direction for your own team(s). YOU must deliver the results day-in and day-out.

Levels of Management

Top Managers

Middle Managers

First Line Leaders

Sleeping giants, many alarms apply to you -- wake-up alarms, emergency alarms, and daily calls for attention. So whether you're in a nightmare, a gentle dream, or simply a daydream, it's time to wake-up and be the LEADER your organization needs.

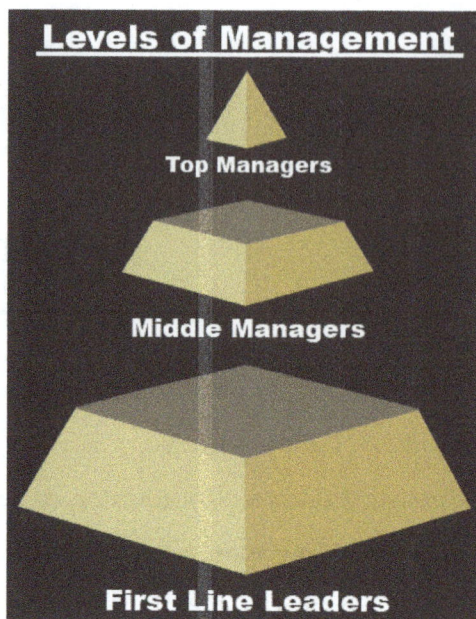

What is an Effective FIRST LINE LEADER?

Hailing All First Line Leaders!

Effective management is all about achieving organizational goals and results -- effectively and efficiently -- with the support of others.

First Line Leaders (FLL) exist in all organizations, and should be seen as GIANTS in the organization. Why is the world of the giant so important?

- FLL frequently interface with the end-users of the organization's products and/or services.

- FLL make daily management and leadership decisions that impact 50-70% of their organization's members.

- The organization's members often decide whether to stay or leave, solely based on how their FLL treat them. Good or bad, people will always judge their giants.

In order to succeed, FLL will have to interchangeably perform the duties of a manager and a leader. FLL who are effective ensure their vital organizational role when they work from a foundation of knowledge and skills that help serve them and their team members.

Effective managers

Plan, organize, and control resources.

Effective leaders

Are focused on people.

But how do you ensure that you are effective? By using what we like to call a LEADER model, FLL will grow to be the giants their organizations most need.

The LEADER model stands for:

- **L**earning: acquiring knowledge about yourself and your team member(s)

- **E**xpectations: identifying and communicating clear expectations

- **A**ction: demonstrating accountability for appropriate actions and results

- **D**evelopment: reinforcing continuous self and team growth

- **E**ngagement: committing to and actively supporting organizational needs

- **R**ecognition: providing on-going acknowledgment of contributions

When giants act in collective and unified alignment, using the LEADER model, a synergistic advantage is brought to the organization. All FLL who become LEADER giants help others grow and thus *leverage* the full team potential to better benefit from collective capabilities and contributions. This clearly presents a potential workforce *multiplier effect* within organizations. By leveraging the collective potential of all FLL, *positional advantage* -- or competitive advantage -- is secured within the organization.

LEADER giants follow the LEADER model because it makes their job easier and their team(s) more effective. When giants leverage their collective talents, the organization benefits by: improved customer service, end-user satisfaction, enhanced quality, improved performance, increased flexibility, increased productivity, and lowered costs.

We fully recognize the enormous complexity of Management and Leadership as a field of study and application. The 6 elements of the LEADER model provide a foundation for FLL to build on. From this strong foundation LEADER giants can firmly entrench and improve their management and leadership skills in the organization. Effective giants enjoy the advantage of seeing further, and are better at connecting with others because they effectively perform in their expanding spheres of thought, work, and influence.

4

Section I: Learning

Part 1

How can you help others, if you can't first help yourself?

Once upon a time a young, newly hired Department Head, with little previous management experience (Melissa - FLL), was becoming increasingly frustrated with the performance of one of her workers (Tom). Melissa believed that Tom had personal shortcomings; he repeatedly did not follow her directions, and appeared to have an attitude problem because he would ignore her. She started to think Tom didn't want to take orders from a woman. Melissa, now very angry, wanted to reprimand Tom by issuing a written performance-warning notice. This notice would result in Tom being terminated if no changes occurred.

Fortunately a LEADER giant challenged Melissa's thinking by simply asking, "How well do you really know Tom? Is there something you're missing that is impacting his ability to follow your instructions?"

Although Melissa didn't want to give Tom the time-of-day at this point, she realized that she needed to understand Tom better before taking such a drastic performance-oriented step.

Melissa started by watching Tom from a far to see how he interacted with customers. Often while working in an aisle, customers would call out to Tom and he would blatantly ignore them. Melissa was infuriated and flustered, but she noticed that he ignored both men and women equally. This got her thinking that Tom did not necessarily have a gender issue with her, but rather something else was at play. With a little more observation, she noticed Tom only ignored customers when his back was turned or he was not facing them directly. Melissa was not a great detective but she put two and two together. She went and checked with appropriate company authorities on Tom's personnel file, and it was soon discovered that Tom was hearing impaired.

Melissa took the initiative and found out whether the company could help with paying for a hearing aide. Once she knew what resources she could bring to bear on improving the situation, she had a meeting with Tom to address her concerns and offer suggestions.

Although this was a difficult conversation for Tom, he admitted to his hearing shortcoming and how he thought he had successfully compensated for it. When Tom realized how his co-workers and customers perceived him; he felt embarrassed and disheartened.

Fortunately, he wanted to remedy the situation right away and agreed to wear a hearing aide. It turned out that Tom needed two hearing aids and the company helped him with both. Tom is currently one of Melissa's best workers and when she needs something done, he is her go-to person for the job.

A Giant Initial Insight

From Melissa's story we can identify that she needed to recognize within herself her own gender bias. She incorrectly anticipated men would struggle with taking orders from her. This led to a poor initial assessment of the Tom situation.

She also learned that she needed to be patient with her workers, because she's prone to rushing to take action. She didn't apply patience by doing her homework, and didn't communicate with Tom to get more information and feedback about what she thought she saw as the problem.

As a manager and a leader you have the responsibility to **guide, develop, and support** your team members. You ensure individual team member success and organizational success. This is a huge undertaking! Here's how huge the undertaking truly is:

1. The LEARNING process takes time and is ongoing. You will never reach an end-point of LEARNING. Experience is acquiring knowledge over time – so realize that time is your ally. Sleeping giants don't gain quality experience but rather sleepwalk through time. If Melissa were a sleeping giant she would have hastily issued a written performance-warning notice to Tom. As a sleeping giant she would have most likely repeated this action with other team members in other situations – to the detriment of all. Sleeping giants repeat actions without analysis or thought; hence, there is no time or reflection to support LEARNING in the sleeping giant's

world. LEADER giants actively reflect and think about situations as they pass through time, and become more efficient problem solvers and effective communicators by LEARNING from both mistakes and successes.

2. LEARNING starts with the giant. There has to be LEARNING of self before there can be team member LEARNING. Strong self-knowledge promotes heightened awareness, sensitivity, and understanding of people within situations. You can only effectively impact the performance and success of others on your team when you first understand yourself. Sleeping giant Melissa was not prepared to consider Tom's perspective on her problem. Melissa rushed to the conclusion that Tom was biased against females. Sleeping giant Melissa had limited evidence from her personal interaction only, which led to her generalization that Tom is a misogynist. LEADER giant Melissa self-reflected on her own gender bias and was big enough to overcome her own prejudice. Her LEARNING resulted in analysis of her own assumptions, which were faulty. When LEADER giant Melissa allowed time for reflection and accurate data collection, she was better prepared to address the true issue at hand – Tom's hearing loss.

3. LEARNING expands from the LEADER giant to the TEAM. By applying LEARNING to yourself you can model for your TEAM -- that is leading by example. Your ability to walk-the-talk positively impacts your ability to coach and work more effectively with your team(s). Sleeping giant Melissa would rather have fired her problem away than deal with it. LEADER giant Melissa was able to discuss and handle Tom's situation with empathy, development, and support. Tom could have responded negatively, and he may have been fired as a result. But LEADER giant Melissa created such a helpful environment to address Tom, he responded as a LEADER team member by welcoming her coaching. LEADER giant Melissa's initial investment of time in self and then her team, has resulted in the reward of a happier and more productive team member environment.

So why don't sleeping giants wake-up to LEARNING?

Based on our experience in working with many managers and leaders, we are continually surprised with how little people personally know about themselves. The answers we typically hear include:

"I thought my job was about working with others – and not about me!"

Bill (FLL) from Illinois, USA

"My managers have never focused on this – so why should I?"

Sally (FLL) from Texas, USA

"Self-assessment is difficult to do, and takes a lot of work and time – which I don't have!"

Janice (FLL) from Birmingham, England

"I am afraid to know. I may not like what I learn and find out about myself – so why do it? Better to avoid."

Dinesh (FLL) from Bangalore, India

"I wouldn't know where to start with self-assessment?"

Carlo (FLL) from Rio de Janeiro, Brazil

These are more alibis than valid reasons for not doing self-assessment and thinking about self first and team members next.

Self-assessment and reality checking serves as an invaluable beginning point for management and leadership success. Sleeping giants may not be aware of factors like learning preferences or styles, learning opportunities, and learning environments. The "Get Real" Learning checklist will help all giants (re-) inform their knowledge about LEARNING.

The "Get Real" LEARNING checklist:

1. *How do I learn, and what is my preferred learning style?*

Understanding your own preferred learning style could be extremely helpful in support of LEARNING, both for yourself, and for those with whom you frequently interface.

- If you learn best by hearing/listening, you are an *auditory* learner.

- If you learn best by seeing/sight, you are a *visual* learner.

- If you learn and remember best by doing/hands-on, you are a *kinesthetic* learner.

Learning

You may find one of these learning preferences to be your dominant learning style or you may be a blend of learning styles. What is most important to realize is that learning is best done as something active and engaged.

Learning styles describe the way team members approach LEARNING, as well as the types of LEARNING experiences in which they feel most comfortable. If sleeping giant Melissa just handed Tom a written performance write-up, then there may have been no further learning but rather a firing. In LEADER giant Melissa's coaching she needed to teach in a private one-on-one setting for it to be effective with Tom. This empathy and understanding of how Tom might best receive personal information about his shortcoming, best allows for Tom to learn and react constructively.

Psychology teaches us that the best way to retain knowledge, apply processes, or enhance critical thinking, is by being able to teach others what you have learned. Learners concretize knowledge when they internalize, demonstrate, and apply the knowledge by teaching it to others. This includes practice by doing and role modeling all that you do. By creating effective LEARNING environments that incorporates ideas of teaching others and practicing-by-doing, LEADER giants are able to leverage their team members' LEARNING exponentially. Team members fall asleep in front of their sleeping giants in a world of lectures or PowerPoint torture.

2. *How do I become my own best learning advocate?*

Giants also need to understand and appreciate the importance of being your own best advocate to help benefit yourself, first and foremost. Take personal accountability for your own LEARNING. Learn as much as you can about yourself, by reflecting on your LEARNING (meta-cognition), and gaining feedback from others about your LEARNING. It takes courage and insight to speak up for your own best LEARNING interests. Giants should be courageous – LEADER giants are courageous.

3. *Where do I look for places and opportunities to support my LEARNING?*

Remember that LEARNING opportunities -- for yourself and team members -- occur every day on-the-job. One of your most powerful LEARNING environments is your actual work environment, a great learning laboratory available to you and all of your team members. Learning to leverage LEARNING -- organization wide -- is the ultimate benefit that

LEARNING can bring a team, a work unit, or a total organization. Don't get complacent and lazy; LEADER giants are always LEARNING and don't have time to sit down and rest.

A Giant final insight

Many people have different learning needs. People tend to learn differently from each other for a variety of reasons including: interest, readiness, and learning profile. Unless a First Line Leader understands and responds to those differences they will fail many of their team members. In the final analysis, each team member needs to be thought of as an individual learner who requires the benefit of your energy, your heart, and your mind.

In effect, by being a student of yourself and then a student of your students, you will help to ensure total LEARNING, best performance, and team success.

Part 2

Acquiring knowledge about yourself and your team member(s)

(L-1) The Personal Action Plan for Self document forces reflection in support of LEARNING for performance improvement. LEARNING is the means by which the FLL increases awareness and understanding of a subject. This tool allows you to identify priority areas as determined by reality or need. Here are some examples of general categories that many giants find they can improve upon: communication, leadership, commitment, recognition, and teamwork.

On the form (L-1) we provide you with a leadership example. The LEADER giant Melissa wants to acquire feedback from team members about her leadership strengths and weaknesses. The example elaborates on how she breaks that LEARNING need into manageable steps that will result in the desired outcome – understanding her strengths and weaknesses so that she can protect and improve on them respectively.

LEARNING

(L-1) FLL: Personal Action Plan for SELF

Name: _____   Date: _____

Rank your preferred learning styles from best (1) to worst (3)?

☐ Auditory   ☐ Kinesthetic   ☐ Visual

Identify 3 action areas that support LEARNING about SELF. Model your 3 answers to match our example below.

Learning Area(s) to work on	Key action step(s)	Specific timeline(s)	Key resource(s)	Desired outcome(s)
Gain feedback about strengths and weaknesses as a leader to build and improve on.	STEP 1: Create annonymous system, administrator collects data. STEP 2: Analyze data STEP 3: Share with TEAM STEP 4: Change behavior(s)	ST 1: 1 week. ST 2: 1 week. ST 3: 1 week. ST 4: x weeks.	Boss, self, & administrator Self Self & TEAM Self & TEAM	Strengths protected, weaknesses addressed. Behavioral changes.

Learning Area(s) to work on	Key action step(s)	Specific timeline(s)	Key resource(s)	Desired outcome(s)

Learning Area(s) to work on	Key action step(s)	Specific timeline(s)	Key resource(s)	Desired outcome(s)

Learning Area(s) to work on	Key action step(s)	Specific timeline(s)	Key resource(s)	Desired outcome(s)

Learning

 (L-2) FLL: Assessment by TEAM Member document has each team member assess his or her understanding of the key job duties he or she performs. The form then checks to see whether the understanding of key knowledge and key skill areas align with the key job duties. This alignment assessment is done by the FLL once the form has been completed. At this stage, the FLL leader might probe the team member for additional understanding and clarity. The form also requests that the team member identify knowledge or skills that require improvement, and lastly, what learning obstacles may currently impede progress.

The example provided on the form (L-2) relates to the story of Melissa and Tom. The example is specifically targeted to help the FLL understand the concept of LEARNING before expecting his or her team member(s) to participate in the process. Your team member(s) will not be aware of the story, but that should not inhibit the understanding of what is required on the form.

LEARNING

Please thoroughly reflect on each question before writing your answers. Complete this form in private. Be prepared to discuss your answers with your team leader.

Team member name: _____

Position: _____

Date: _____

Key job duties: (List your five main duties only.)

E.g. In-store customer service.

1. _____
2. _____
3. _____
4. _____
5. _____

What do you think is the key knowledge required for each duty:

E.g. In-store customer service - product knowledge.

1. _____
2. _____
3. _____
4. _____
5. _____

What is the key skill or ability requirement for each duty:

E.g. In-store customer service - sales skills.

1. _____
2. _____
3. _____
4. _____
5. _____

What key knowledge and/or skills do I need to improve?

E.g. Closing the sale better.

1. _____
2. _____
3. _____

Can you identify any major learning obstacles you may have?

E.g. I get distracted by noise which hinders my listening.

1. _____
2. _____
3. _____

Part 3

Extending LEARNING from self, to team member(s), to TEAM

LEADER giants – you should now combine your knowledge of self with your knowledge of your team member(s) to leverage better LEARNING for the benefit of the TEAM. During Part 3 you will be exposed to the successful practices of other LEADER giants. You do not have to reinvent the wheel or forge ahead on your own to leverage LEARNING.

Practices for LEADER giants:

1. Feedback

LEADER giants realize that feedback is nourishment. Feedback occurs both within the giant via self-reflection, and externally from outside sources. Remember Melissa's story, where she first assumed that Tom was sexist. Her feedback to self was faulty. When her feedback source was tested by reality checking with a fellow LEADER giant, she was able to LEARN appropriately.

Feedback often comes to LEADER giants in the form of criticism. Bitter criticism may be difficult to swallow but often results in dramatic LEARNING. Sweet criticism may be kind to the palate, but may not really be genuine in praise, and may not affect real LEARNING. Giants are prepared to cultivate a taste for feedback (criticism and coaching) because they realize LEARNING is revitalizing.

Get fat on feedback. Good or bad, regardless of the intent or the source – accept and welcome the feedback. One "No thank you," from the giant often limits the buffet of future offerings.

2. Reflection

LEADER giants should look in the mirror each day, and take stock of the ground covered that day. Pick a time of day and environment that best suits you to gain maximum illumination of the day's events. This can be done in private or discussion with another LEADER Giant. Remember Melissa's insight gained by the probing of another LEADER giant?

When reflecting, consider key events or recent outcomes, and identify at least 1 key insight gained from that illumination. This reflection should inform future sharing and implementation with others. To retain ideas, consider using a personal diary or journal log for assistance. For LEADER giants your daily reflection should be, "Mirror, mirror on the wall teach me LEARNING that benefits all."

3. Arrivals

When a stranger visits your home for the first time, it is polite to engage them in conversation that is focused on them. In much the same way, a new team member should be treated accordingly. LEADER giants should treat new team members with total civility and respect. Think of all the new knowledge that can be LEARNED, especially from an external new hire. A new team member tends to bring a fresh perspective, a new set of experiences, and potential objectivity that he or she often presents naively, freely, candidly, and constructively.

The LEARNING that occurs in these situations is often exponential in relation to time. Tire out your new team member with dialogue; don't let them sleep. When he or she is engaged in telling you about his or her ideas and experiences, your interest and involvement also helps to better assimilate the new team member into the team for the benefit of the TEAM.

4. Departures

Team member(s) can die, be fired, retire, resign, transferred, or promoted. Team member(s) do in fact leave organizations. Take the time to listen thoughtfully to the reason(s) a team member might offer for electing to leave – unless they die on you.

Also seize the opportunity to ask the team member for any feedback or suggestions they care to offer you personally. Understand that although this might be a difficult conversation, it is necessary that you probe for real LEARNING. You may be surprised with the candor and honesty offered.

Learning processes for teams in the organization:

Once you understand the value and importance of LEARNING PRACTICES, you need to figure out how to weave LEARNING into your organization's day-to-day functioning. There is no hard and fast rule for how best to do this, but there are four general processes that should be incorporated into your organization's work routines.

1. Brainstorming, and sharing of best practices:

Identify a LEARNING issue or need for your organization. FLL should aim to identify key topics in advance of meetings, thus allowing attendees to prepare and present their thoughts for a deeper and more meaningful learning exchange. Invite all appropriate team members to share first-hand knowledge and experiences about the identified issue or need. In the course of listening to all expressed experiences and suggestions by others, you can begin to identify some possible alternatives to help address the LEARNING issue or need.

2. Distill your learning for team members:

While attending training seminars and conference events there is an abundance of knowledge presented. Prioritize your LEARNING by identifying only one or two key areas of content that you can teach and thoroughly train to your team members. Not everything presented at a seminar has applicability – be discerning.

As a LEADER giant you are most likely to want to stride ahead during training. Realize that you more than likely have grasped the LEARNING quicker than your team members are able to grasp the content. There are many reasons for this: experience, interest, learning style, passion, and commitment. A 2-hour seminar may be all that the LEADER giant requires to understand the material, but in reality the re-teaching could take significantly longer with team members. Be patient. If you teach correctly and patiently at first, you will not need to re-teach remedially at a later stage.

3. Applying content mastery

Learn in depth every aspect about the topic you intend to teach. Your mastery provides you with confidence and allows others to learn from you so they too can teach with confidence. To assess your success as a teacher have the team members re-teach the topic material to other team members or back to you. In this way you can assess for understanding and evaluate the effectiveness of your own teaching ability. Once team members have successfully demonstrated their ability to teach and apply the content acquired, they can then be held accountable to the new standard demonstrated through their own teaching.

4. Learning assessment

How do you evaluate the LEARNING after the implementation of a major program, training, or project? You need to review and reflect on: what was planned, what occurred, what failed, and what was deemed successful. The best LEARNING occurs when FLL take the time to reflect on both breakdown(s) and achievement(s). LEADER giants fully capitalize on LEARNING when they reflect on both failure and success.

Section II: Expectations

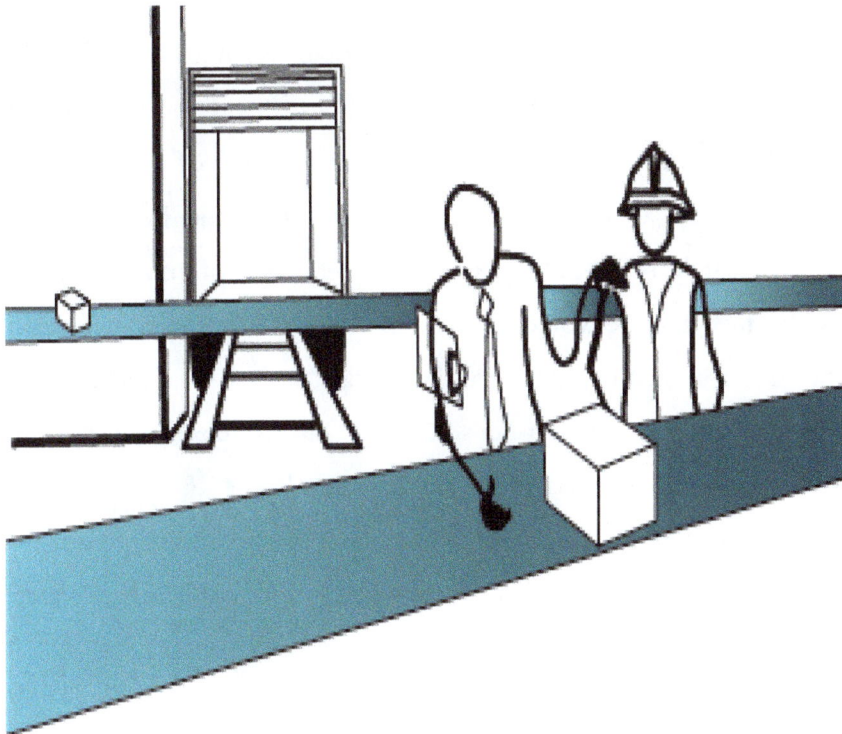

Part 1

Expect the best, prepare for the best, and demand the best – always manage EXPECTATIONS

Once upon a time, Jackson (FLL) was an experienced Operations Supervisor at a district distribution center. His team was enrolled to attend the company wide 2-day long computer scheduling and logistics training program. One of his team members (Ian – Scheduler) said he would attend, but cancelled at the last minute because of a sudden bout of flu. Jackson immediately rescheduled Ian for the very next offering in the district, and once again Ian reconfirmed that he would attend. For the second time, at the very last minute, Ian cancelled once again by taking a personal day citing family issues. Jackson was very surprised and disappointed when he learned of Ian's behavior. Ian was clearly setting a behavioral pattern that did not meet with Jackson's vision for his TEAM.

Jackson at his earliest opportunity confronted Ian to identify the real underlying issue concerning the training, and to find a satisfactory resolution for all parties concerned.

JACKSON: What's going on here Ian?

IAN: Do I really need to do this training? I'm already proven and experienced.

JACKSON: All team members need to attend regardless of individual experience. You'll learn the new knowledge and develop skills that the company has identified which will benefit you and our team.

Ian released a deep, loud sigh that got Jackson very, very worried.

JACKSON: Ian, I sense that there is something deeper going on here that you're not telling me. What are your concerns -- what are you worried about? What are you not telling me?

IAN: Look, I'm afraid that I won't be able to hold my own in the class with everybody. It's been 30 years since I last had to learn from a book, and that didn't go so well. Other guys look up to me right now, and if I don't do well they won't respect me the same way. That's very important to me.

JACKSON: Ian, you're one of our most knowledgeable, experienced, and top performing guys at our site. This training is going to make you even better, and nobody will know how you perform in the training exercises. You need to really do it. The company is not allowing any exceptions. I know you're going to do better than you think you will, purely if for no other reason based on how you currently perform at our work site. I'm very proud of the work you're currently doing.

LEADER giant Jackson demonstrated initiative by proactively seeking information directly from Ian to help resolve the issue. Jackson demonstrated compassion and empathy in a realistic appraisal of the situation and what was required from Ian.

Reluctantly, Ian did attend the next training offering. He contributed a great deal during the training especially once he realized how experiential and hands-on the training was. Ian later entered Jackson's office rather sheepishly for their follow-up meeting.

IAN: I don't often like to admit when I'm wrong, but thank you for sending me to the training. I got a lot out of it, much more than I thought I would.

JACKSON: I'm very happy to hear that Ian.

IAN: Well the other reason I'm here is that I actually want to serve as the senior site-scheduling coordinator that was talked about during the training. Can we make that happen for this upcoming year?

JACKSON: I'll support that happily, especially given your work reputation.

A Giant Initial Insight

Jackson's understanding of management and leadership meant that he clearly made a distinction between daily work tasks and work planning (long-term) of team member contributions. For LEADER giants, work planning is an essential Key Responsibility Area (KRA) and reinforces teamwork culture within the organization.

Jackson's leadership vision guided his EXPECTATIONS and reinforced a culture of open engagement without blame. The rightful focus during discussion was on understanding Ian's issues as opposed to affixing blame. Jackson's intent was always to address the situation and not get lost in finger pointing. Jackson knew how best to deal with a team member who was resistant to LEARNING and EXPECTATIONS due to Jackson's own prior experience, training, and reflection in dealing with similar situations. Unbeknownst to Ian, Jackson identified Ian's problem as an issue of lack of self-esteem.

Ian's insecurities concerning LEARNING environments jeopardized his good standing with Jackson and the TEAM. LEADER giants must challenge themselves and their TEAM to be successful, especially since many giants and team members have the human tendency of being resistant to change.

Jackson emphasized that the EXPECTATION was non-negotiable and necessary to enhance Ian's skill set. Jackson then set about pointing out all the reasons why Ian was likely to be successful in the training. This interaction modeled EXPECTATION setting that was clear, positively framed, with reality checking at all stages of the process.

As a manager and a leader you have the responsibility to:

- Articulate expectations clearly
- Reinforce expectations positively
- Manage expectations realistically

So why don't sleeping giants wake-up to EXPECTATION setting?

Based on our consulting experience with organizations, we continually hear FLL reiterate the themes of apathy for setting EXPECTATIONS. Many sleeping giants will defend their apathy for EXPECTATION setting with statements like the following:

"It's so very clear to me what to do because it's just common sense. But you should see the blank stares I get, the lights don't ever seem to be on."

Bill (FLL) from Philadelphia, USA

"I explain it to them, but then when it comes to them demonstrating the key behaviors, what do you think happens -- Nothing! 'Cause they're incompetent."

Gareth (FLL) from Grangemouth, Scotland

"They take a whole day to train me, but then they give me all of four hours to teach my team."

Yolanda (FLL) from Mexico City, Mexico

Similarly, team members often contend that position duties, responsibilities, and tasks are not stated clearly, positively, or realistically.

"I'm asked to do everything and anything, but it's never clear what's really important or matters most."

Janet (team member) from Boston, USA

"He calls me 'dumbass' because I mess up on something I've never been trained to do, and you wonder why I don't have a better attitude with this guy. I hate him so much."

Saravanan (team member) from Bangalore, India

"She never gives me enough time to do the job properly, and when I want to make changes she tells me, 'Now is not a good time.' – but there's never a good time for fixing things in her world."

Jorgen (team member) from Stockholm, Sweden

With virtually no clarification or reinforcement from their sleeping giants, team members often feel incompetent, uninspired, unsuccessful, and frustrated. All giants need to remember that people find it difficult to approach other people with their concerns and issues - let alone sleeping giants who still need to be woken up. No one wants to wake a sleeping giant known for having a grumpy temperament upon waking.

A Giant final insight

Each team member brings a range of knowledge and skills to the team, along with a variety of personal needs and support issues. A LEADER giant needs to understand and appreciate those differences. Differences are valued and respected, but at the end of each day all team member(s) must be aligned with the mission, vision, and purpose of the TEAM.

The performance bar of EXPECTATIONS needs to remain high for everyone at all times. Every day on-the-job you will help support team member self-esteem, growth, performance contributions, and your overall team's success.

As a LEADER giant you will only get what you plan for. Expect the best, prepare for the best, and demand the best – always manage EXPECTATIONS.

Part 2

Setting EXPECTATIONS for self, then TEAM, then team members

EXPECTATIONS for self

The LEADER giant first sets EXPECTATIONS for himself or herself. Don't expect to hold others to a high standard until you yourself meet the standard(s) you set. Your EXPECTATIONS are then often couched in terms of your vision for the TEAM and team member(s). Vision must have a moral component, guiding principles, and a planning mindset.

The moral component relates to doing the right thing, which is taking care of people in a way that promotes safety and legality.

Guiding principles serve the organization and TEAM with thoughts and behaviors that direct daily operations. Principles include themes like end-user satisfaction, continuous learning, and respect for all.

The planning mindset refers to translating the moral and guiding principles into a message that is clearly communicated and understood by all team members – this is your leadership vision.

Key responsibility areas (KRA) for the LEADER giant exist at 2 levels: the level of the LEADER giant expectations for self, and the level of expectations for TEAM.

LEADER giant self-expectations checklist (Refer to Example Form ES-1 to guide you.):

1. Know your 3 key responsibility areas: work planning, people planning, and teamwork (culture) planning.

- Sleeping giants guess or don't care about what needs to be worked on. They either go through the motions like somnambulists or put-out-fire reactionaries. Sleeping giants drift into areas that may not be important to the TEAM or organization.

- LEADER giants take initiative to effectively communicate and align with management. This action clearly defines the scope and depth of what the LEADER giant is responsible and accountable for. By checking in with management in this way, there is also clarity about what EXPECTATIONS management has for you.

2. LEADER giants purposefully articulate LEADER KRA OBJECTIVES and goals with clarity for their own use and the benefit of their TEAM(S).

- Sleeping giants may talk in their sleep, but that doesn't mean they will remember what they've said. Sleeping giant's communication is random and accidental.

- LEADER giants follow clear steps and provide direction to guide the work of TEAM(S) and team member(s).

3. LEADER giants identify and focus on essential BEHAVIORS that will consistently support them in the delivery of KRA and objectives.

- Sleeping giants have a one-behavior cycle: sleep, wake-up to put out a TEAM fire, and return to sleep to recuperate.

- LEADER giants consistently demonstrate essential key behaviors. The behaviors support the objectives, which support the KRA. Everything is linked and aligned which allows the LEADER giant to walk-the-talk.

Expectation Setting EXAMPLE

(ES-1) FLL: Leadership EXPECTATIONS for SELF

FLL name: _Jackson_   Date: _01/10/2012_

3 Key Responsibility Areas (KRA) for leadership of SELF.

WORK PLANNING: of team KRA, objectives, and essential behaviors.
PEOPLE PLANNING: of individual team member KRA, objectives, and essential behaviors.
TEAMWORK (CULTURE) PLANNING: Team/individual behavioral norms.

Objective Setting Stage   ☐ 3 months   ☑ 6 months   ☐ 12 months

Work Planning Objective
TEAM KRA are identified, communicated, implemented, and monitored for ongoing progress.

People Planning Objective
Team member KRA are identified, communicated, implemented, and monitored for ongoing progress.

Teamwork (Culture) Planning Objective
TEAM and team member behavioral norms are identified, communicated, practiced, and monitored for ongoing progress.

Essential behaviors supporting KRA / Objectives

Behaviors: WORK PLANNING
i. _End user focused and oriented - the end user drives all work decisions._
ii. _Results oriented - take ACTION to bring about planned results._
iii. _Prioritization - First order work tasks and then dive in to complete them._

Behaviors: PEOPLE PLANNING
i. _Self-advocacy, ownership, initiative - you are accountable for your ACTIONS._
ii. _Continuous LEARNING - cultivate life-long-learning habits in all you do._
iii. _Development minded and growth - protect strengths and address weaknesses._

Behaviors: TEAMWORK (CULTURE) PLANNING
i. _Two-way communication - open, honest, respectful, and trusting._
ii. _Problem solving - based on issues and not blaming people._
iii. _Coaching and mentoring - all team members are resources to each other._

EXPECTATIONS for TEAM

Now let's focus on the KRA level of EXPECTATIONS for TEAM. Alignment of EXPECTATIONS is an ongoing process -- this is very similar to LEARNING. EXPECTATION setting becomes easier when it becomes a daily habit; until then, it is the LEADER giant's continual clear, positive, and realistic reinforcement of EXPECTATIONS that propels the TEAM forward.

EXAMPLE

(ES-2) Alignment of TEAM responsibilities

FLL: Step 1

FLL lists all key responsibility areas (KRA) for the team.

1. Ordering
2. Scheduling
3. Invoicing
4. Shipping
5. Reporting

Refer to Jackson and Ian's story.

FLL: Step 2

FLL identifies which team members are responsible for providing appropriate support in each KRA.

1. Ordering 2. Scheduling 3. Invoicing 4. Shipping 5. Reporting	2. Scheduling 3. Invoicing 5. Reporting	1. Ordering 2. Scheduling
Jackson (FLL)	Ian (Team member)	Sally (Team member)

FLL: Step 3

Summarize and analyze the information in a meaningful way. Below are two possible examples.

This is a Venn Diagram that visually displays where there are overserviced areas (2) and underserviced areas (4).

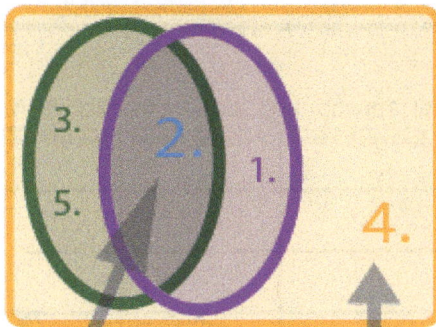

Overserviced responsibility area

Underserviced responsibility area

This is a Matrix or Table that visually displays where there are overserviced areas (2) and underserviced areas (4).

Key Responsibility Areas	FLL	Ian	Sally
1.	✓		✓
2.	✓	✓	✓
3.	✓	✓	✓
4.	✓		
5.	✓	✓	

Overserviced responsibility area

Underserviced responsibility area

FLL & Team: Step 1

FLL shares this preliminary document with the TEAM to confirm that all KRA have been identified, and that responsibility has been appropriately assigned.

- Assign to Sally key responsibility area #4. Shipping. Provide Sally with one week's training to effectively learn this area. Sally must then report back and teach FLL.
- Re-evaluate key responsibility area #2. Scheduling regarding the need for all three team members to support this area. Note: Ian has asked for total responsibility for scheduling.
- Reprioritize all key responsibility areas for FLL so that it is clear to team that FLL provides an oversight role that is not detailed support.

FLL & Team: Step 2

One-on-one meetings with team members to complete Form (ES-3).

31

Expectation Setting

(ES-2) Alignment of TEAM responsibilities

FLL name: _____

Date: _____

FLL: Step 1

FLL lists all key responsibility areas (KRA) for the TEAM.

1. _____

_____

2. _____

_____

3. _____

_____

4. _____

_____

5. _____

_____

FLL: Step 2

FLL identifies which team members are responsible for appropriate support in each KRA.

KRA	FLL	Team member name	Team member name	Team member name	Team member name	Team member name	Team member name
1.	✓						
2.	✓						
3.	✓						
4.	✓						
5.	✓						

FLL: Step 3

Analyze data for overserviced and underserviced KRA. Reassign responsibilities as needed.

FLL & Team: Step 1

FLL shares this preliminary document with the TEAM to confirm that all KRA have been identified, and that responsibility has been appropriately assigned.

FLL & Team member: Step 2

The FLL then has a one-on-one meeting with each team member to complete Form (ES-3) Assessment with TEAM MEMBER, and team member signs off on responsibilities.

EXPECTATIONS for team member(s)

The LEADER giant with team members should jointly set high mutual standards of EXPECTATION, resulting in a feeling of challenge, excitement, and commitment. At this stage, the LEADER giant will guide alignment where all team member(s) understand EXPECTATIONS. In some situations a FLL may need to be prescriptive and be more directive with EXPECTATION setting. LEADER giants - use your discretion and good judgment.

There will be hiccups and casualties along the way. New team member(s) will need to be brought up to speed to match the high expectation(s) for the TEAM. Also realize that departures from the TEAM could result in re-aligning responsibilities and key objectives for the remaining team members.

EXAMPLE

(ES-3) Assessment with TEAM MEMBER

Team member name: _Ian_
First Line Leader name: _Jackson_
Date: _01/22/2013_

3 key responsibility areas (KRA).

i. _Scheduling_
ii. _Invoicing_
iii. _Reporting_

List each job objective for each KRA.   ☐ 3 months ☐ 6 months ☐ 12 months

i. _To develop and confirm **schedules** based on end user requirements._

ii. _To send **invoices** to end user 1 week prior to service delivery._

iii. _To generate timely, comprehensive, and accurate **reports**._

Identify the key behavior(s) team member will demonstrate to accomplish each objective.

i. _**Schedules**: 1. Forecasting reliability of schedules. 2. Interfacing with end user's schedule and needs. 3. Communication skills: Strong interpersonal skills._

ii. _**Invoicing**: 1. Accuracy of document. 2. Timely generation. 3. Accurate record keeping._

iii. _**Reporting**: 1. Communication skills: Excellent writing skills in report generation. 2. Analysis and problem solving skills: Ability to interpret data and act on information in a timely manner. 3. Customer oriented: Strong interpersonal relations with client counterpart._

Team member signature: _____

First Line Leader signature: _____

Part 3

Extending EXPECTATIONS from self, to TEAM, to team member(s)

LEADER giants – don't be overwhelmed. The EXPECTATION setting stage is very often responsible for creating sleeping giants, because giants would rather avoid the hard work of planning out a leadership vision for their TEAM.

To aid your conceptual understanding of EXPECTATION setting, include the 2 points below in your thinking. You do not have to reinvent the wheel or forge ahead on your own to leverage EXPECTATIONS:

Practices for LEADER giants:

1. Line-of-sight EXPECTATIONS

As a LEADER giant you need to understand how you personally impact and support the key goals of your organization. Knowing what and how you contribute to the success of your organization in terms of your job is known as *line-of-sight*. Once you clearly understand your own line-of-sight it is incumbent upon you as a LEADER giant to help your team members' identify their own line-of-sight. When a team member knows his or her line-of-sight it provides better: work challenge, buy-in, commitment and team effectiveness.

2. Setting end-user EXPECTATIONS

Periodically invite key external and internal end-users to attend your team meeting(s) to share and exchange their views of what is important to them as end-users. Listen generously for understanding and clarification.

Section III: Action

Part 1

Walk your talk. Actions are your words when you are a positive role model

Once upon a time, a newly delivered refrigerator wasn't making any ice. Mr. and Mrs. Wallace, the now not so proud owners of the expensive appliance, wanted immediate resolution. The Wallace's were repeat customers and expected that their loyalty would prompt quick action from the store.

In the store at the customer service department, team member Carla received the Wallace's call. Carla pulled the Wallace's purchase history up on her computer and noticed a long history of complaints about faulty appliances.

If you could see Carla's expression you would have seen her eyes roll as she thought, "Here we go again." Carla was ready to dismiss the urgency of the situation, especially ….since it was 11:56 am…. she was hungry, and her lunch was scheduled to start at noon. As a result, Carla explained to the Wallace's that she would need to pass their issue along to her supervisor Anthony. She also told the Wallace's that Anthony was not presently available and would call them later on in the afternoon.

Carla had a great lunch. When she returned she passed on the Wallace's information to Anthony (FLL). Anthony, who had been present the whole morning, noted the time of the Wallace's call and asked Carla why she didn't deal with the issue before lunch. Carla shrugged. Anthony knew that this was a great teachable moment and opted for a positive resolution instead of reprimanding Carla for her lack of urgency and responsiveness towards customers.

Anthony asked Carla to sit in on his call with the Wallace's. The Wallace's were polite although somewhat frustrated at having to wait for a return call. Anthony listened intently and allowed the Wallace's to say all they needed to say. Anthony then started asking insightful questions about the appliance to try to determine whether the problem lay with the installation or the manufacturer of the appliance.

Anthony wanted to problem-solve the issue over the phone as was customary, but by now the Wallace's wanted no part of that and were asking for a replacement product. Anthony politely asked the Wallace's whether he could pay them a visit to inspect and problem-solve the appliance that afternoon.

Anthony took Carla with him because he wanted her to experience how good it felt to provide great customer service. His thinking was that if Carla experienced true customer satisfaction resolved by her own timely efforts, the joy of having done a job well in this instance would hopefully carry over to other customers.

Carla knew how to service all the appliances sold in their store due to prior training. She often had to talk customers through the problem-solving processes she had learned. During the drive over to the Wallace's, Anthony coached Carla on how she was going to resolve the Wallace's problem while he watched. Anthony would gladly add assistance if needed but wanted Carla to take leadership concerning her call.

At the Wallace's, Carla was a great communicator explaining to the Wallace's each step of her problem-solving process as they explored the problem of the faulty icemaker. It turned out that the freezer thermostat adjustment dial had been incorrectly set during the initial installation.

The Wallace's were thankful and relieved that the appliance was not faulty. They were also pleasantly surprised with the personal attention given to them by the store TEAM. From initially thinking that they had received bad customer service, the Wallace's ended the day thinking they had just received the best customer service ever from any company.

Upon return to the customer service department, Carla talked enthusiastically to everybody about the call she and Anthony had just serviced. It was the first time that Carla had ever personally met with customers. That really hit home with her - she was helping people and not just voices on the phone.

Shortly before the end of the day, once Carla had calmed down from all the excitement of earlier, Anthony called her into his office to discuss the positive outcome.

This short time delay allowed for more reflection by Carla to realize the importance of her impact in customer service and reaffirm her *line-of-sight*.

Anthony proved to be a LEADER giant in this situation because he offered great coaching by walking-the-talk, solving the problem with great urgency, and allowing Carla to own her own actions.

A Giant Initial Insight

Anthony was sensitive to the ***urgency*** of the Wallace's complaint. Anthony coached Carla on taking initiative by first seeing if she could LEARN by sitting in on his call. When it was clear that a call would not be enough, Anthony escalated his level of service to turn what could have been the loss of a long standing customer into a triumph of service resolution.

Anthony demonstrated a ***can-do positive attitude*** during his coaching of Carla, as well during the conversations with the Wallace's. His even temperament was always aimed at solving the problem and helped the situation. Anthony made a conscious decision to not blame or reprimand Carla. Instead, he showed her respect while modeling appropriate behavior, which encouraged Carla to in turn show the utmost respect to the Wallace's in person.

Although Anthony did not personally resolve the problem at the Wallace's house, he assured Carla that he was a safety net if needed. He could have directly ***walked-the-talk*** and solved the problem himself, but Anthony's decision to shadow Carla proved even more productive as it demonstrated trust in her ability to succeed. Anthony ensured that he was visible, present, and accessible at all times.

Lastly, Anthony ensured that the LEARNING of the ACTION steps was consolidated at the end of the day. He allowed Carla time for reflection and time for the success of the call to sink in, before calling her back into his office to confirm what she had learned by her ACTION.

So why can't sleeping giants rouse themselves into ACTION?

It takes energy to apply ACTION. ACTION requires thinking and active participation. Sleeping giants may avoid taking ACTION for numerous reasons. Some sleeping giants avoid ACTION simply because they are afraid of how they will be judged by people. Fear is fantastic at driving sleeping giants deeper under the covers into the fetal position to avoid ACTION. Lack of knowledge or skills may also drive sleeping giants under cover for fear of being viewed as incompetent.

We frequently hear team members muttering many of the same things about their sleeping giants:

"Just wait it out, and even he will get tired of his 'new idea'."
Francis (team member) from Singapore

"You can mouth-off or just do what you want, and no one gives a damn."
Jermaine (team member) from Camden, USA

"So I'm expected to work through lunch, but it's okay if she's away for two hours during her lunch break. That's totally unfair!"
Jenny (team member) from Oslo, Norway

Often sleeping giants struggle to turn this negativity around, or are not even aware of it, or worse yet condone it.

LEADER giants inform all their ACTIONS with 4 guiding principles.

1. *Walk-your-talk (Role-modeling)*

LEADER giants, you must deliver on what you say you will do - every day. Every giant step you take is noticed. Your credibility suffers when your words do not match your actions. Once your credibility is lost it is virtually impossible to regain. You need to consistently and visibly demonstrate personal accountability for your own actions.

Effective role modeling supports your integrity. Team members will most likely copy your actions and not your talk. For example, when you make a mistake in judgment, decision making, or take a wrong action as a giant; be honest and openly acknowledge the error with your team members. Let them know what was learned, what will be corrected, and what will be done differently going forward.

Action

When a LEADER giant visibly and consistently demonstrates high standards for personal accountability day-in and day-out, it actually becomes a lot easier to do the same with team members. This creates a strong culture of accountability.

2. Sense of urgency

ACTION is active. When you have a great awareness of where your EXPECTATIONS are set, you should prime yourself to catch your team member(s) living EXPECTATIONS. In the few instances that they don't meet EXPECTATIONS, you must react with urgency to immediately correct the breakdown of their EXPECTED behavior. The longer you let issues persist the more likely they are to become bad habits that you condone. Time is of the essence in every situation.

3. Can-do positive attitude

This principle is strongly grounded in reality. Nobody trusts or follows a positive fool or a can't-do sleeping giant. Problems are difficult to solve and raise stress levels for all participants. The LEADER giant who persists with an even temperament, and relates to every situation with a positive (but realistic) outlook, infects all team members with a positive-resolution sense of purpose.

4. Reflection

ACTION is instant and immediate in many circumstances, but ACTION without reflection is like shooting without aiming. It's important to be able to pull the trigger, but if you don't stop to check that you've hit the target, how can you recalibrate for your next shot.

There will be times that you take ACTION and it will have been the wrong ACTION. The process of reflecting on how you proceeded through an ACTION forces you back into a LEARNING cycle that might have you adjust your EXPECTATIONS. Regardless of whether reflection confirms your ACTION taking or points out further problems – this stage promotes growth.

A Giant final insight

Everyone needs to pull their own weight and be responsible and accountable to achieve planned results. Ultimately we are all measured by the actions we take and do not take. Our actions always speak louder than our words. A Giant needs to be in tune with the actions and contributions of his team members, and also absolutely first needs to demonstrate actions with urgency. A fast moving Giant is an impressive thing to behold.

You should use every opportunity to provide strong, positive, consistent role modeling on-the-job for all team members to observe and emulate. Walk-your-talk. Lead by your example. Show your team how best to act. This is putting your best foot forward.

Part 2

The LEADER giant takes ACTION

Dreaming about ACTION doesn't alter reality for sleeping giants. LEADER giants improve on reality with ACTION. <u>(A-1) FLL: Monthly reflection of SELF</u> document focuses on the LEADER giant and his or her ACTIONS. We recommend the FLL uses this document once a month.

There are four guiding principles that support ACTION: Walk-the-talk, sense of urgency, can-do positive attitude, and reflection. You will assess your own performance of ACTION taken from both a quantitative (frequency) and qualitative (effectiveness) perspective on these guiding principles.

Once you have established trust with your team, you may elect to extend this tool to your team members by having them anonymously rate you. This will ensure team member candor.

Establish a culture that promotes ACTION by involving your team members when they see your EXPECTATIONS of SELF, relating to ACTION. Here team members will experience transparency and help you to stay transparent in your daily dealings with ACTION. This is great for improving and sustaining organizational culture.

EXAMPLE

(A-1)FLL: Monthly Reflection of SELF

Name: _Anthony_   Year: _2012_

☐ Jan ☐ Feb ☐ March ☐ April ☐ May ☐ June ☐ July ☐ Aug ☐ Sept ☐ Oct ☑ Nov ☐ Dec

1. Walking-the-talk

How frequently am I walking-the-talk?

○ Never ○ Sometimes ○ Often ☑ Always

Behaviors I like:
Very accessible to team members.
Talk consistently about objectives.

How effectively am I walking-the-talk?

○ Poor ○ Fair ○ Good ☑ Excellent

Behaviors to improve on:
None.

2. Sense of urgency

How frequently do I apply a sense of urgency?

○ Never ○ Sometimes ☑ Often ○ Always

Behaviors I like:
Focus on the customer – Home visit, same day.

How effectively am I applying a sense of urgency?

○ Poor ○ Fair ☑ Good ○ Excellent

Behaviors to improve on:
Instill higher sense of urgency in team member ACTIONS.

3. Can-do attitude

How frequently do I apply a can-do attitude?

○ Never ○ Sometimes ○ Often ☑ Always

Behaviors I like:
Carla has mirrored my positive behavior based on coaching.

How effectively am I applying a can-do attitude?

○ Poor ○ Fair ○ Good ☑ Excellent

Behaviors to improve on:
None.

4. Reflection

How frequently do I reflect on ACTION taken?

○ Never ○ Sometimes ○ Often ☑ Always

Behaviors I like:
Coached LEARNING opportunity real time with the ACTION.

How effectively do I reflect on ACTION taken?

○ Poor ○ Fair ☑ Good ○ Excellent

Behaviors to improve on:
Too soon to tell. Watch Carla's calls over the next week to check for application of LEARNING.

Part 3

What is your ACTION legacy?

Words without ACTIONS are daydreams. When you say, "I'm on it!" Commit to ACTION right away. Do it expediently. People remember delayed, unfulfilled, and empty ACTION. People also remember immediate and effective ACTION. What is your ACTION legacy?

Section IV: Development

Part 1

Personal improvement and growth benefits everybody

Once upon a time, Lei (FLL) was hired as a college Adjunct Professor for a local college. Lei was enthusiastic and eager, and wanted to shine for her students so that it would be the best English Composition course her students had ever taken. She was especially nervous because she had never taught before and desperately wanted development to ensure that her teaching skill would match her enthusiasm.

Lei met with the head of the department (Andrew – FLL) and received her textbooks for the course. When Lei asked for some guidance on how to best teach her course, Andrew offered her a syllabus from the previous semester and instructed her to follow that. Lei realized that this was the only help she was going to receive from the department head. It was clear that this was a sink or swim situation – not a very reassuring picture.

During the first week of teaching Lei quickly realized the limitations of her own teaching experience as student interest waned. She thought it best to solicit the help of other experienced instructors and tracked down two other Composition instructors who were amenable to having Lei observe them. After 4 hours of observation and 2 additional hours of post-observation discussion, Lei now had a more practical, structured, and focused approach to her own classroom teaching style. Her students showed slight improvement in their writing ability but were still, for the most part, disengaged from the whole process.

One day as Lei looked out over her class while they were going-through-the-motions-of-writing she realized that her students should also really be giving her continuous feedback about her own teaching effectiveness. Student inputs would most likely generate better enthusiasm and motivation for writing, as well as improving her teaching effectiveness.

Lei spent a week mulling over what would be the most effective way to gain this feedback in support of her development, yet would be sincere and constructive. She decided on a technology solution because her students had self-reported that they used a lot of technology like email. Lei created a simple Google Form that asked a few questions, such as: Please rate my teaching effectiveness this week (1-10), what I liked best about your teaching was, what I liked least about your teaching was, and I think you can improve as a teacher by.

Lei also allowed for students to answer the form anonymously. Every week she would send out the form to her students and she would then receive email updates every time a student responded. This feedback from the students was invaluable. Lei quickly calibrated her lessons to incorporate more group activities and ensure a higher degree of interactivity. Her feedback rating also steadily improved as she listened to her students and applied their suggestions. By the end of the semester Lei reflected on her progress as an instructor, and was clearly able to point to areas of development that helped contribute to her success as a first year adjunct. Both Lei and her students greatly benefited from this process.

A Giant Initial Insight

Some organizations internalize DEVELOPMENT as part of their organizational culture and recognize it as part of a formal strategy to be accomplished with organizational resources during work time. Other organizations require you to DEVELOP with your own resources on your own time. Without DEVELOPMENT you certainly are not going to improve in your current position or worse yet, stagnate. Regardless of your reality, DEVELOPMENT must be planned for and be ongoing. Regardless of whether your organization recognizes the value of DEVELOPMENT you still need to decide on whether you will be a sleeping giant or a LEADER giant.

We all need to take primary ownership and accountability for our own DEVELOPMENT. In a TEAM setting the FLL should take the initiative in first improving himself or herself. This DEVELOPMENT ACTION then is positively role modeled for your team members who should recognize it as part of you walking-your-talk. In the Lei story, Andrew should have started DEVELOPMENT with himself and then had a DEVELOPMENT plan for his team members like Lei. However, because Andrew made it clear that he did not value DEVELOPMENT, Lei took the initiative and struggled through different approaches to DEVELOP her skill as an adjunct professor.

Development

We all have personal strengths and weaknesses to build on and improve. Lei realistically assessed her own teaching early on and concluded she had weaknesses that needed to be addressed as DEVELOPMENTAL opportunities. To her credit, she identified multiple sources for further DEVELOPMENT. She observed experienced instructors to try to model their best practices, and she solicited feedback from her students that was ongoing. Lei used this data to create DEVELOPMENT tools that helped improve her classroom instruction, which benefited the students in their LEARNING.

DEVELOPMENT whenever possible should take place on-the-job. DEVELOPMENT should not be divorced from real-world environments. The work environment is the most fertile ground for growth and DEVELOPMENT every day. Recognize though that DEVELOPMENT should be planned for, monitored, and measured to assess ongoing progress. Without a structured DEVELOPMENT plan your learning will be haphazard, random, and without focus.

So why don't sleeping giants seek DEVELOPMENT?

Although sleeping giants may think of their dreams as a form of DEVELOPMENT, there is nothing actively being done during their dreaming. Development takes an awareness that only comes from effectively performing ACTION – and we all know how sleeping giants feel about ACTION. In discussing DEVELOPMENT with sleeping giants, we often hear more reluctance and apathy:

"Who's going to develop me – let alone me developing others?"
Barry (FLL) from Chicago, USA

"My top performers already know all that they need to know, and I just fire my bottom performers if they don't get it."
Donna (FLL) from Santa Barbara, USA

"I don't have the time, money, or energy to develop team members. Who does?"
John (FLL) from Dallas Fort-Worth, USA

"If I give you the job, then you must be able to do the job. I can't let you fool around and mess with my customers because you're learning. Training you in front of my customers is just embarrassing."

Lao (FLL) from Tokyo, Japan

"My boss couldn't smell development if it hit him in the face – he wouldn't get it if I did anything for my own people."

Jorge (FLL) from Rio de Janeiro, Brazil

The key to beginning effective DEVELOPMENT for both yourself and your team members is gaining an accurate, realistic assessment of your overall strengths and weaknesses. Make sure that your thinking starts with your current position responsibilities, actual performance, key behaviors, and promotion potential – when warranted. Coaching and feedback from others helps you to gain clarity relative to your strengths and weaknesses.

Consider developmental resources that are already at your disposal: reading material, special projects, task force work, committee participation, temporary assignments, job rotation, coaching and mentoring, on-the-job training, classroom training, off-site visits, and presentations to team members. This is not an exhaustive list. Many of these ideas and tools are not expensive – be creative.

A Giant Final Insight

Sleeping giants think DEVELOPMENT is an option or a luxury; but often when they wake up to reality, the performance bar has been raised without them realizing it. They are now at a competitive disadvantage. Don't be caught napping.

Raising the performance bar is a continuous process that applies to everybody. DEVELOPMENT ensures no team member is left behind. LEADER giants see their competition clearly and recognize that DEVELOPMENT provides competitive advantage, job satisfaction, superior performance, and team effectiveness.

Your goal as a LEADER giant is to get things done, but you must continually get better at doing it. By building on your own knowledge and skills, you get better at performing your job. By helping team members build their knowledge and skills, they get better at performing their jobs. All of this benefits the TEAM and the organization.

51

Part 2

Creating DEVELOPMENT planning for SELF and team members

The LEADER giant needs to gather realistic data from multiple sources to get a well-rounded picture of his or her strengths and weaknesses. There is a lot of *politically correct speak* within some organizations around the term 'weakness', which may be referred to as deficiencies, developmental opportunities, gaps, or areas to address. We believe our LEADER giants have egos that can handle the word – weakness. LEADER giants are interested in honest, realistic, and descriptive feedback of their performance, because they recognize that they are constantly growing and improving.

(D-1) FLL: Developmental Feedback is a document that should be handed out for completion twice a year. Hand the document to all people who are best able to provide relevant input on your knowledge, skills, and abilities. These typically are people who have consistent engagement with you in the course of your work duties. This may be your immediate manager, team members, peers, FLL, customers, end-users, or suppliers.

Prior to handing out these forms, gain the support of your immediate manager. Try to involve your immediate manager in this process by asking him or her to hand deliver the forms to identified people. When your immediate manager hands out the forms, it increases the seriousness of the feedback, and it ensures buy-in from your immediate manager.

Try to get feedback from at least 5 sources. The more data you collect, the more complete will be the picture of your current knowledge, skills, and abilities. Don't be afraid to ignore statements that appear to be outliers. If a comment is repeated, then you know to mark that strength as something that should be protected going forward. If a repeated comment is a weakness, then that should be considered an area for DEVELOPMENT.

The data captured at this stage will serve you as a foundation for completing a more formal, holistic DEVELOPMENT plan that we will help you create in document D-2.

EXAMPLE

(D-1) FLL: Developmental Feedback

FLL name: *Lei*   Date: *11/25/2012*

Feedback relative to knowledge, skills, and abilities in my current position.

Please provide me with your input concerning how you view my personal strengths and weaknesses relative to my job knowledge, skills, and abilities. Please remain anonymous, but leave detailed feedback. If you could note at least 3 strengths and 3 weaknesses with examples for each, I'd be very appreciative. Thank you in advance. When you have completed this form please send it to: *The English Department*
Attention: Beckie Sims (Administrative Assistant) Building Ten Floor Four.

For each section there is a feedback example to help guide your responses.

Strengths with explanation or example(s):

Great enthusiasm - everytime she enters the classroom she's smiling and animated. It's very stimulating and inspiring.

Pride with the desire to improve - She constantly pushes herself to be the best at all she does.

Great with feedback - She actually was interested in what we thought about her teaching style. And we could see that she really took our comments to heart.

Weaknesses with explanation or example(s):

Lacks experience - It's clear that she's still figuring out how she needs to teach. She keeps changing how she teaches because she keeps seeing better ways to do things, but it's frustrating because there is no rhythm or flow to what she's doing.

Lacks confidence - at times it's clear she doesn't know what she wants to do. It's then that she seems to waiver in her teaching and I found that frustrating. I want to know my professor knows what she is doing.

Response time - She is often slow getting our grades back. I'd like more constructive feedback explaining the grade I received. Both for good or bad grades.

Please return this document within a week of receiving it.
Thank you again for your help in my DEVELOPMENT plan.

(D-2) Individual Development Plan document is aimed to create an individual DEVELOPMENT plan to be reviewed and updated every 6 months. Take all your data from (D-1) to identify your 4 most prominent strengths and 4 most prominent weaknesses. The form will then require you to select 2 areas of strength and 2 areas that are DEVELOPMENTAL opportunities to protect and improve on respectively. Lastly, the document will require longer-term DEVELOPMENTAL projections, relative to positions of interest, projects and committees.

Once the document has been completed, it should guide your ACTIONS for the next 6 months. Remember it is not enough to only work on your DEVELOPMENTAL opportunities, but you must protect the strengths you already possess.

EXAMPLE

(D-2) Individual Development Plan

Name: _Lei_   Date: _12/02/2012_

Summary of key strength(s) and key developmental improvement opportunities

STRENGTHS:
- Self improvement focused.
- Coachable and feedback oriented.
- High energy and enthusiasm.
- Content knowledge is broad and strong.

DEVELOPMENTAL OPPORTUNITIES:
- Lacks teaching experience.
- Moments of inconsistent confidence.
- Lacks sense of urgency - grading.
- Limited peer network.

Strength to leverage: (Be specific)	Protection Plan/ Training Action(s)	Timeline/ Target Date(s)	Result(s)
Self improvement focused.	Model self improvement for students with teacher writing samples.	Daily/every class.	Students become more critical of their own writing.

Strength to leverage: (Be specific)	Protection Plan/ Training Action(s)	Timeline/ Target Date(s)	Result(s)
Content knowledge is broad and strong.	Write a research paper for publication.	By 06/2013 date for publication in academic journal.	Publication.

Developmental opportunity 1: (Be specific)	Development Plans/ Training Actions	Timeline/ Target Dates	Results
Lacks teaching experience.	Time on the job, with reflection.	Ongoing.	Better teaching practice with time (based on feedback and evaluation.)

Developmental opportunity 2: (Be specific)	Development Plans/ Training Actions	Timeline/ Target Dates	Results
Limited peer network.	Introduce yourself to English Comp faculty. Identify possible mentor. Join Internet social group for Comp.	End of Jan (2013).	Known by faculty. Bi-weekly mentor meetings. Contribute monthly to social group.

Future positions, assignments, projects, and committees of interest:

Tenured full time professor (2015).

Longer term interest in being the department head (2018).

Represent school in the local chapter of a Reading Association.

Part 3

Unleash DEVELOPMENT – release the stranglehold within your TEAM

LEADER giant – value your DEVELOPMENT, even if your organization doesn't -- yet. DEVELOPMENT demands focus and attention! This is where you leverage your LEARNING, EXPECTATIONS, and ACTION into a plan for growth.

To aid your conceptual understanding of DEVELOPMENT consider utilizing the 3 points below:

Feedback

Share your key findings with your immediate manager and TEAM(S). Thank them for their anonymous feedback, and share with them what you plan to do. This will help to hold you accountable for your actions.

Initiate a similar feedback process with any of your team members, based on need, and based on priority. Make sure that all of your team members understand this can be done for any of them – but it will require their personal voluntary support and respect for confidentiality of all information provided. An appropriate Individual DEVELOPMENT Plan will then need to be implemented by the team member to address the findings and to support appropriate action.

Mentoring

Establish and encourage participation in a mentoring process for your team members. The LEADER giant can serve as a mentor for others, or team members can serve as mentors for peer team members. Depending upon the size of the department, you may just do it within the department itself, or you can seek additional mentoring opportunities from larger teams in other departments.

Development

Team Knowledge and Skill Enhancement – Role Rotation

Assign and rotate team member roles in support of the ongoing growth and development of your team. The broader the skill-base of every team member, the stronger your team will be.

Assign a team member to act for you in your absence, assign and rotate different roles for your team during staff meetings (i.e. note-taker, facilitator, presenter, timekeeper, etc.), prepare your team members for their roles in advance and hold them accountable for the role assignments.

Sleeping giants are bottlenecks because they don't share skills and experiences. People want to strangle something when they experience a bottleneck. Don't let your TEAM look for something to strangle - it may turn out to be you.

Section V: Engagement

Part 1

People best support what they help to create – involvement drives ENGAGEMENT

Once upon a time, Jose (FLL) was a 10-year veteran Sales Manager for a medical instrumentation company of 150 employees. He was responsible for managing a 6-member sales team. The company's top priority was to provide the best customer service in their industry.

A key way to support that initiative, Jose thought, was by achieving outstanding sales results. Jose wanted his team to be the best -- the best in the region, and then the best in the company. He quickly developed a customer sales vision and plan for his team. His EXPECTATION was that the TEAM would execute and deliver on the plan immediately.

He identified 3 main actions for his sales team:

- Each sales member needs to exceed his or her sales target that is currently pegged at 10% over the previous year's sales performance.

- Each sales member needs to make 20 new customer contacts per month via telephone.

- After each customer contact, each sales member needs to generate a sales contact report and file it within twenty-four hours.

Jose got very fired up over his new plan. He thought it was a fantastic challenge for his team members, and Jose interpreted his plan as addressing the issue of increasing awareness, passion, and commitment within his sales team.

Jose flew into ACTION. Over the course of the next quarter, with each month's sales results failing to meet Jose's new targets, Jose became increasingly frustrated and antagonistic to all around him. With particular wrath being paid to his team members.

Jose's boss, Belinda (Sales Director), had heard rumblings from other employees about Jose's curt and sarcastic turn for the worst. Belinda decided to quickly focus on both the downturn in projected sales and employee complaints before the next quarter started.

In the meeting, when Belinda engaged Jose, Jose spilled forth like a released pressure cooker. Belinda listened empathetically and ultimately asked Jose:

BELINDA: Whose sales vision and plan was this Jose?

JOSE: Mine of course, who else!

BELINDA: That's my point. You are not a team of one Jose. Last time I looked there were 6 other people on your team.

JOSE: But I'm the leader...

Jose caught himself. There was a long awkward silence, and Jose really thought about what had just been said. Belinda knew not to say anything, but let Jose process his comment.

JOSE: Wow!

BELINDA: Wow what Jose?

JOSE: It never dawned on me that my plan was MY plan and not the plan of all of us. No wonder they hate me now. Oh NO.

BELINDA: Slow down you don't have to overreact. You can talk this through with your team. They still respect you and want to perform for you and themselves. I know you are all an ambitious lot.

Jose had a lot to digest and left the meeting with a new frame of mind to *reach out* to his team. Involvement was the new name of the game and Jose worked diligently with his team to reach mutually set standards. The team agreed on 3 new challenges:

- Being that the company was just coming out of the great recession, it was more reasonable to expect a 5% increase in sales over the last year.

- Sales members agreed to make 25 new customer contacts per month, but had total freedom in how they achieved their number. This allowed for added communication technologies other than just using the telephone.

- After each customer contact, each sales member needed to generate a sales contact report and file it within forty-eight hours. The team members could also choose between electronic or paper filing, where previously only paper filings were accepted by fax.

Engagement

The three new points looked fairly similar to Jose's original points only these three had everybody's buy-in. When Jose asked whether his team felt energized, passionate, and committed; he received an emphatic YES! Civility returned, commitment spiked, and Jose's team members felt like they could talk with him once again.

This LEARNING and EXPECTATION setting led to the ACTION that ultimately met the new goals. Everybody felt good, starting with Jose. Over the course of the business year the team was recognized as the top regional sales team, and was also recognized as the top company team.

A Giant Initial Insight

To err is human, and to LEAD takes time.

When LEAD-ER giants ENGAGE their TEAM(S) it's sublime.

LEAD on your own, which is what a sleeping giant does, and you will err. A LEAD-ER giant needs to get results of the people, by the people, and for the people. The bottom line for Jose is that ENGAGEMENT permeates everything the TEAM does, and when a FLL tries to do the heavy lifting alone – failure is inevitable. Many FLL burn out their muscles because they carry the weight of the TEAM without the support of team members. Everybody must be involved in ENGAGEMENT and committed to the TEAM. Commitment is all about the level of buy-in of each individual team member.

However, the LEAD-ER views ENGAGEMENT from 2 perspectives. The first perspective is the starting point for every LEAD-ER giant because it involves role-modeling ENGAGEMENT at the highest level of commitment (conviction). The expectation is that team members will strive to perform at this level of ENGAGEMENT.

The second perspective is that the LEAD-ER giant assesses how ENGAGED the TEAM is with the LEAD-ER giant. The subtle distinction here is that we are looking at ENGAGEMENT from the bottom-up. In this second perspective the LEAD-ER is assessing to what degree are the team members buying into the process and culture (TEAM). Once the LEAD-ER knows the commitment level of each team member, the LEAD-ER can then decide whether to reinforce the commitment level or develop the commitment level of each team member.

For the LEAD-ER giant, ENGAGEMENT must always exist at both perspective levels. Keep one giant eye on how you role model the highest commitment (conviction in all you do) and be critical of yourself. Use your other giant eye to assess each team member's level of ENGAGEMENT. Generously show your TEAM how to be ENGAGED, but also objectively and realistically assess each team member's level of ENGAGEMENT.

The Commitment Spectrum

There are five levels of commitment: awareness, agreement, support, ownership, and conviction. Non-awareness is the lowest level of ENGAGEMENT and does not appear on The Commitment Spectrum, whereas conviction is the highest level of ENGAGEMENT on The Commitment Spectrum. Passion is the means by which a person moves within the Commitment Spectrum. Passion is the different energy levels associated with each commitment level:

> Awareness (lower) = ambivalent energy
>
> Agreement (low) = intrigued energy
>
> Support (high) = eager energy
>
> Ownership (higher) = enthusiastic energy
>
> Conviction (highest) = exhilarated energy

Before the LEAD-ER giant can LEAD his or her TEAM and team members, he or she must embody and role model conviction (1st perspective).

So how do you move team members from awareness to conviction?

When it comes to levels of ENGAGEMENT, LEAD-ER giants may need to start at the very beginning of ENGAGEMENT with certain team members. Don't assume that team members are already ENGAGED.

Step 1: Awareness-testing

For each team member figure out whether he or she has:

- A basic knowledge and understanding of task. Does the team member have the necessary knowledge, skills, and abilities to perform his or her work?

Engagement

- Awareness of SELF-benefits. Can the team member answer, "What's in it for me?" Although this may seem selfish, it is where initial buy-in starts.
- Does the team member know what to work on and how to prioritize his or her work?
- Have I made my TEAM expectations explicit to the team member?

Step 2: Activating awareness

LEAD-ER giants activate awareness in the team member by:

- Being a stimulating role model using passion (exhilaration) to ENGAGE team members (1st perspective).
- Identifying what triggers and exhilarates each team member into the highest level of ENGAGEMENT (2nd perspective).
- Creating a TEAM culture of vigilant awareness (2nd perspective).

Step 3: Moving towards conviction

Commitment builds and takes time. Recognize that and stay the course with your focus, consistency, and positive reinforcement. Realistically stretch and challenge team member thinking and behaviors at periodic intervals.

Step 4: Approaching conviction for team members and the TEAM

Sleeping giants are not present and have little idea about their team members. As a result the TEAM tends to drift apart and dissipate. Physics teaches us that to gather momentum we must accelerate mass. The sleeping giant's TEAM often breaks apart, and does not gain momentum because there is no mass to accelerate.

The LEAD-ER giant harnesses and aligns all team members to a TEAM vision. This creates mass and when this mass is accelerated, it creates a TEAM trajectory towards success. For the LEAD-ER giant commitment is positive momentum.

Here are ways to help instill, sustain, and drive commitment:

- Continually welcome team member ideas, inputs, and suggestions (2nd perspective).
- Periodically review with team members the benefits of accomplishing an initiative (2nd perspective).

- Always catch your team members being committed, and then praise that behavior (2nd perspective).

The Commitment Spectrum is both a conceptual and a coaching tool. In this tool, ENGAGEMENT is pervasive and permeates LEARNING, EXPECTATIONS, ACTION, and DEVELOPMENT (LEAD). Although RECOGNITION has not yet been discussed, be aware that it too is tied to ENGAGEMENT and pervades and permeates LEAD. Although RECOGNITION is present in the tool, it will not be the focus of discussion at this point.

The Commitment Spectrum

Engagement

Guide for SELF & team member coaching

Commitment Level	LOWER AWARENESS	LOW AGREEMENT	HIGH SUPPORT	HIGHER OWNERSHIP	HIGHEST CONVICTION
Commitment Level Descriptors	• Ambivalent	• Intrigued	• Eager	• Enthusiastic	• Exhilarated
	• Basic knowledge, understanding of task.	• Agreement of responsibilities.	• Idea, input, suggestion exchange.	• No excuses/no alibis.	• Total buy-in with strong belief.
	• Aware of self benefits.	• Alignment of self and team benefits.	• Tentative start.	• Can do.	• Will do.
	• Leader directed.	• Leader guided.	• Leader and team-member monitored.	• Team member owned.	• Team member enforced.
	• What to do.	• How best to do.	• Do it.	• Review what's done.	• Learn and build on what was done.
Desired Outcome	Initial understanding/ acceptance	Role clarity/alignment of purpose	Active participation/ involvement	Personal accountability	Exhilarated and totally engaged
Questions of SELF and Team Members	• Level of awareness?	• Clear on purpose, role-responsibilities, objectives, goals, and key duties?	• Gain teammember ideas, inputs, and suggestions?	• What is working and not working?	• Key learnings and insights communicated?
	• Level of understanding?	• Clear on manager expectations?	• Feedback on actions taken?	• What can be done better?	• What will be improved, leveraged, and sustained?
	• Knowledge, training needed?	• How will teammember and team benefit?	• Monitoring line-of-sight impact?	• Barriers and roadblocks addressed?	• Shaping line-of-sight impact?
	• How will teammember benefit?		• Clear on contributions and impact?	• Correcting line-of-sight impact?	
Focus Area(s)	Learning	Expectations	Action	Action Development	Development Engagement
	Recognition				

A Giant final insight

LEAD-ER giants are relentless about results and believe in partnerships with their team members. LEAD-ER giants want positive momentum and create it by exhilarating team members to do a great job, feel a connection to their TEAM, and believe that their contributions add value.

When you have conviction, everything starts to be fun. Work that is experienced as fun becomes something that you love to do. Who doesn't want to love what they do? Think how powerful it is to unleash that potential and create that culture.

Part 2

Tools for Levels of ENGAGEMENT

(Eng-1a and Eng-1b) Level of Team Engagement is a tool for gathering data on ENGAGEMENT.

(Eng-2) The Commitment Spectrum Applied is a tool for assessing and identifying trends of team member levels of commitment.

On the example tools, we have used the story of Jose to illustrate how effective each tool is. Had Jose used these tools it is likely that he could have avoided a troubling 3rd quarter of sales results and the embarrassing and humbling meeting with his Sales Director, Belinda.

EXAMPLE

(Eng-1A) Level of TEAM ENGAGEMENT

FLL Name: _Jose_   Year: _2012_

Complete this form bi-annually or quarterly. ☑ Half year   ☐ 1st Q   ☐ 2nd Q   ☐ End year   ☐ 3rd Q   ☐ 4th Q

Wholistically rate your TEAM on their current level of committment concerning each Guiding Principle. When rating, stress objectivity and realism in your assessment. Inflated scores make for a faulty tool.

Learning

Commitment Levels

Question	1 Lower (Awareness)	2 Low (Agreement)	3 High (Supportive)	4 Higher (Ownership)	5 Highest (Conviction)
Does the TEAM take responsibility for LEARNING?	☑				
How attentive are my team members to their personal LEARNING style?			☑		
What is my TEAM's level of continuous LEARNING?		☑			
Do my team members LEARN from each other?			☑		
Do team members use their work environment to aid their LEARNING?	☑				

Expectations

Commitment Levels

Question	1 Lower (Awareness)	2 Low (Agreement)	3 High (Supportive)	4 Higher (Ownership)	5 Highest (Conviction)
Do team members consistently set high standards for performance?	☑				
How clearly, positively, and realistically do team members communicate?		☑			
Do team members use two-way communication?	☑				
What is your TEAM's level of expectation planning?		☑			
What is your TEAM's level of surprise avoidance and making assumptions?	☑				

Action

Commitment Levels

Question	1 Lower (Awareness)	2 Low (Agreement)	3 High (Supportive)	4 Higher (Ownership)	5 Highest (Conviction)
What is the TEAM's level of responsibility and accountability to achieve results?	☑				
What is the team members level of being visible, present, and accessible to the TEAM?		☑			
What is the TEAM's level of sense-of-urgency?		☑			
What is the TEAM's level of can-do attitude?		☑			
What is the TEAM's level of reflection on ACTION?	☑				

EXAMPLE

(Eng-1B) Level of TEAM ENGAGEMENT

FLL Name: _Jose_   Year: _2012_

Complete this form bi-annually or quarterly.
- [✓] Half year
- [ ] 1st Q
- [ ] 2nd Q
- [ ] End year
- [ ] 3rd Q
- [ ] 4th Q

Wholistically rate your TEAM on their current level of committment concerning each Guiding Principle. When rating, stress objectivity and realism in your assessment. Inflated scores make for a faulty tool.

Development

	Commitment Levels				
	Lower (Awareness)	Low (Agreement)	High (Supportive)	Higher (Ownership)	Highest (Conviction)
What level of ownership and accountability do team members take for their DEVELOPMENT?	1 ✓	2 ☐	3 ☐	4 ☐	5 ☐
How attentive are team members to their strengths and weaknesses?	1 ✓	2 ☐	3 ☐	4 ☐	5 ☐
Do team members perform ongoing DEVELOPMENT?	1 ☐	2 ✓	3 ☐	4 ☐	5 ☐
Do team members DEVELOPMENT within their work environment?	1 ☐	2 ✓	3 ☐	4 ☐	5 ☐
Do team members use multiple resources?	1 ✓	2 ☐	3 ☐	4 ☐	5 ☐

Total the points scored in each LEAD section. Each LEAD section has a maximum score of 25 points.

Learning	10	Expectations	7	Action	8	Development	7

• Identify your 2 weakest LEAD sections based on the total scores above.

    Expectations   _Development_

• Then select and prioritize your weakest 4 to 6 specific TEAM ENGAGEMENT items from the 2 sections identified.

1. _Exp: Do team members consistently set high performance standards?_
2. _Exp: Do TM use two-way communication?_
3. _Exp: What is your TEAM's level of surprise avoidance and making assumptions?_
4. _Dev: What level of ownership and accountability do team members take?_
5. _Dev: How attentive are TM to their strengths and weaknesses?_
6. _Dev: Do TM use multiple resources?_

Now that you have identified your 4 to 6 high priority TEAM ENGAGEMENT items to improve on, next plan to meet with your total TEAM as a group, to clarify and validate appropriate resources, processes, and behaviors as needed.

Engagement

Using the Commitment Spectrum, think holistically about scoring each of your team members in terms of everything they do. Give each team member a rating at the end of every month - evaluate them on the same day for consistency. You should see trends developing that will inform your coaching and DEVELOPMENT in support of your team member. Then use the team member data to plot a TEAM trend. **NOTE: All data should remain confidential and not be shared with team members.**

Thomas
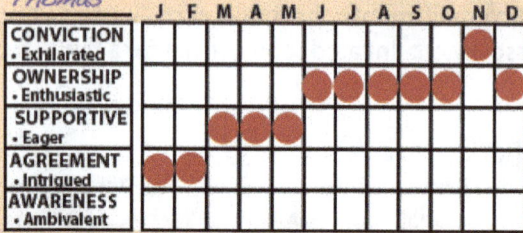

Michael
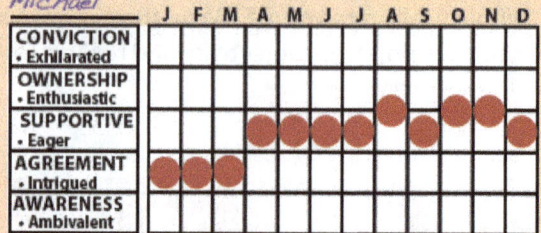

Michelle
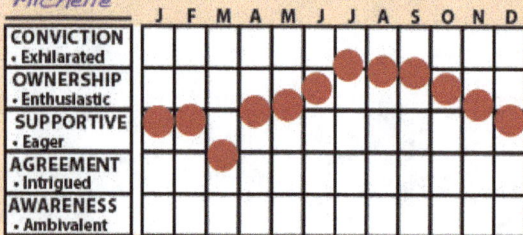

Jorge
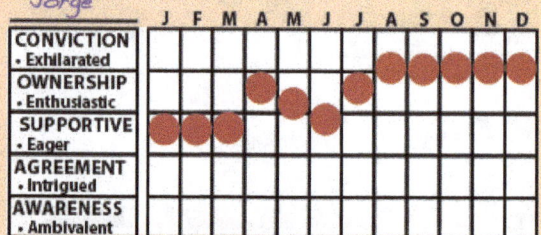

Tanya
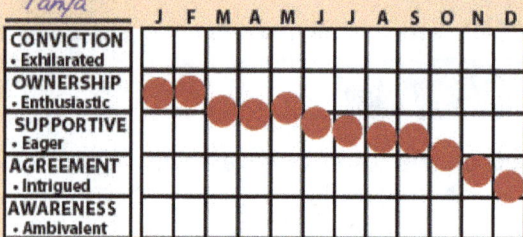

TEAM
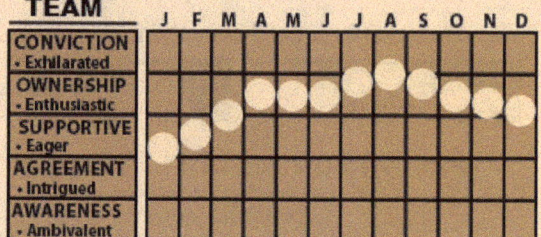

70

Part 3

A Culture of Commitment

Culture is a way of life, and culture is unavoidable. The winds of the world are many, varied, and sometimes turbulently dangerous. Neglect your TEAM culture and the winds will blow away parts of your TEAM. Shape your culture and you can brace against or use the wind to your TEAM's benefit.

For sleeping giants when the winds carry fire, the sleeping giant knows there's a fire only because he or she feels the heat. That's why sleeping giants are forced to react to situations with a TEAM that is uncoordinated and unprepared because ENGAGEMENT is deficient. For the sleeping giant's TEAM, putting-out-fire happens all the time. It is reactive and sadly produces many burn victims. Sleeping giants and their team members are the victims of their own heated emergency culture.

For LEAD-ER giants, chances are a team member is out scouting and alerts the LEAD-ER giant and TEAM that smoke is on the horizon. The LEAD-ER giant then marshals all of his or her resources in a confident, prepared, and well-equipped manner. The LEAD-ER TEAM is able to avoid or deal with the emergency in a timely and effective way. Once the fire has been avoided or put out, the LEAD-ER TEAM makes time to LEARN from the situation. LEAD-ER giants are the shapers of their own ENGAGED culture of commitment.

Section VI: Recognition

Part 1

Take every opportunity to acknowledge your people in their achievements

Once upon a journal, Preetha (FLL) an enthusiastic Safety and Health (S&H) Coordinator, kept an accurate work journal which helped her keep track of organizational issues, events, and actions.

Preetha works with her team of 1 (Ed) who is her assistant Safety and Health Coordinator. Preetha had functional reporting responsibility for all Site Safety and Health Coordinators. She reported directly to Sarah (Group Human Resources Director).

January:
- Self reflection 3rd Jan: Difficult past year performance in S&H (law suit settlement with Occupational Safety and Health Administration - OSHA).
- Group meeting 14th Jan: Sobering but challenging meeting with all division and location site managers. Biggest hurdle going forward might be stopping continued <u>negativity</u> and the absolute need for <u>immediate improvement</u>. Reviewed prior year problems, but also acknowledged all positive things done by sites.
- TEAM meeting and recognition 17th Jan: Thanked Ed (Assistant S&H Coordinator) for his timely collection of positive S&H data for (Jan 14th) meeting (Starbucks gift card given, he really loves gourmet coffee!).
- TEAM meeting 20th Jan: Sarah (Group HR Director) and I recognized site managements' experience and used that experience to set mutually challenging, but realistic goals for the upcoming year.

February:

- Self reflection 4th Feb: Identified criteria for new role - Location Safety and Health Coordinator.

- TEAM action 6th Feb: Worked closely with each site location manager to post new openings. The week of Feb 12th, sites are conducting interviews for qualified candidates. Feb 16th, made selections based on recognizing performance and personal S&H interests.

- TEAM development and recognition 18th Feb: Conducted train-the-trainer S&H program (1 day) rollout with all newly assigned location S&H coordinators. Sarah and I acknowledged and thanked new coordinators for participation at end of day with a group dinner and training program certificates (plus we gave out S&H hats and shirts). Also used training session to test idea for inter-location audit process and gained coordinators' support and buy-in for the audit process.

March:

- Self reflection 5th March: Location S&H coordinators appear to be working well with their site locations. Early, but all seem to be off to a good start.

- Team recognition 7th March: Sent group wide email out to all location managers, acknowledging their support of new S&H coordinators.

- TEAM meeting 9th March: Sarah and I presented audit idea concept at General Manager/Division Manager meeting. All liked idea and collectively set up a working schedule.

April:

- Self reflection 3rd April: Good early Q1 progress made versus group wide S&H goals (all locations met Q1 standards).

- TEAM recognition 4th April: Sent email to all locations acknowledging that first quarter S&H standards were met.

- Self reflection 5th April: Began implementing audit process – no significant problems.

Recognition

- TEAM action 22nd April: Reported out early findings, key suggestions, and acknowledged early audit site results at both group / division level, and site location level.

May:

- Self reflection 15th May: On schedule, making steady progress on all S&H areas.
- TEAM recognition 21st May: Monthly email communiqués acknowledging progress, offering support and thanks.

June:

- Self reflection 15th June: On schedule, making steady progress in all S&H areas.
- TEAM recognition 21st June: Monthly email communiqués acknowledging progress, offering support and thanks.

July:

- Self reflection 6th July: Very good Q2 progress made – all met or exceeded Q2 standards.
- TEAM recognition 21st July: Sent email out to all location managers acknowledging meeting/exceeding Q2 standards.
- TEAM recognition during the week of 25th July: Division managers jumped on bandwagon and each had location food days acknowledging continued success.

August:

- TEAM meeting and recognition 2nd August: Had good teleconference check-in meeting with all location S&H coordinators. No problems shared. All appear very committed and on board, but a lot of work is coming down the pipeline. Acknowledged and thanked them all for their support and contributions in helping group wide safety and health turnaround.
- Self reflection 8th August: Work role demands are forcing me to think about an expanded role for Ed. Possibly coordinator for all location S&H coordinators. Plan to set up meeting to discuss my idea with Sarah.

- TEAM action 24th August: Sarah returned from vacation and set up meeting.
- TEAM meeting 26th August: Meeting with Sarah productive, she is supportive and onboard about increasing Ed's responsibilities. Sarah hinted that I would definitely see more work coming down the pipeline – soon!

September:

- Team member recognition 5th September: Acknowledged Ed's personal contributions and engagement by expanding his role as spokesperson/coordinator for all location S&H coordinators. Means more work and a bump in pay for him. ED accepted happily and thanked me for assignment of new broadened responsibilities.

October:

- Self reflection 6th October: Q3 safety and health results continue to show strong positive directional trends.
- Team meeting and recognition 12th October: Sarah and I reviewed progress with General Manager and Division Vice-presidents and we all went out to a great lunch to celebrate. Made me feel very proud to be recognized and invited to lunch with the VP's.

November:

- Team meeting and recognition 7th November: Sarah invited me to provide updates in person regarding overall S&H performance at Division Manager meeting at Group headquarters. Went very well. Group acknowledgement embarrassed me and caught me off guard.

December:

- Team meeting and recognition 14th December: Sarah and Group General Manager shocked me when they called me into Sarah's office to inform me of my new title: S&H Manager, and their announcement of a new annual S&H scholarship in my honor. It pleased me to no end that they both recognized how much I value S&H education and certification. Really made me feel proud, I can't put it into words. Can't wait to get home to share this news with my family.

Recognition

A Giant Initial Insight

To err is human, and to LEAD takes time.

When LEAD-ER giants RECOGNIZE their TEAM(S), it's sublime.

Team members work in exchange for pay, but team members often don't see money as the be-all and end-all of recognition. Monetary recognition serves a clear purpose that everybody understands, but what's unspoken or not always understood is that people also value non-monetary recognition. Who doesn't appreciate a genuine and timely: spoken "Thank you", a written acknowledgement of excellence, and a meeting that celebrates your hard work.

LEAD-ER giants pay attention to creating a total recognition and rewards system because it ENGAGES team members and reinforces organizational EXPECTATIONS. The LEAD-ER giant must acknowledge and demonstrate to team member(s) and upper management that RECOGNITION works in harmony with ENGAGEMENT.

Consider the model below:

As the LEAD-ER giant it is your job to continually raise your EXPECTATIONS of the team member(s) ENGAGEMENT bar. Your ENGAGEMENT aim is to move your team member(s) from awareness to conviction. In turn, your team member(s) will expect more RECOGNITION for the increased involvement and contributions he or she accomplishes.

As the LEAD-ER giant you need to recognize that the ENGAGEMENT bar is one side of a coin where the RECOGNITION bar is the other side of that coin; hence, the Team member ENGAGEMENT and RECOGNITION bar. Team member(s) may initially increase their levels of ENGAGEMENT without increased levels of RECOGNITION, but sooner rather than later they will become disengaged because their added efforts have not been RECOGNIZED. Half a coin buys nothing.

Sleeping giants think that RECOGNITION is all about money. Therefore, sleeping giants argue that when a team member performs well, there are only two solutions: if you have money, throw it at the team member(s); or if you have no money, withhold all acknowledgment – stay asleep. Sleeping giants promise dream cultures, but all too often deliver nightmare cultures because they do not understand RECOGNITION. Sleeping giants may bluff people into joining a dream TEAM, but when the reality of the nightmare hits, the team member wakes up in a cold sweat – and leaves frustrated and angry!

LEAD-ER giants know that RECOGNITION is both monetary and non-monetary. LEAD-ER giants take on the responsibility of finding out what hot buttons or needs each team member may have in terms of RECOGNITION. The LEAD-ER giant then selects appropriately from a menu of RECOGNITION options that the LEAD-ER giant and organization can provide to create a TOTAL RECOGNITION package specifically tailored to the dreams of each team member(s).

Consider the story of Preetha (FLL), Ed, and Sarah. Preetha was aware that there was more to RECOGNITION than money. Although Preetha used a system more based on her intuition, she had a good understanding of Ed's needs and hot buttons. Were we to unpack Preetha's thoughts concerning Ed, it might look something like the 2 points below:

1. Status is important to Ed.

Consider appointing him as the Spokesperson for all location S&H Coordinators. This will give him high visibility and address his expressed desire to be challenged in the job with a status role.

2. Ed is motivated by peer recognition.

Provide Ed with written feedback from the Train-the-Trainer program for the module he taught. Offer him completed survey responses from the training participants. Ed appreciates feedback as a learning and recognition tool. He can improve on weak areas and feel proud of his strengths as expressed in the survey responses.

Recognition

Point 1 addresses Ed's need for RECOGNITION by first addressing his priority need of status attainment. In this case there was the added perk of a slight monetary increase too. Often RECOGNITION may involve both monetary and non-monetary considerations for promotions or increasing responsibilities within a position.

Point 2 shows that Preetha also confirmed Ed's need for peer RECOGNITION that clearly does not have a monetary component attached to it. The insight here is that when a team member gets closer to an ENGAGEMENT level of conviction, monetary RECOGNITION frequently assumes less importance in the total package of RECOGNITION.

A Giant Final Insight:

LEAD-ER giants should always be thinking about balancing the needs of the individual team member and the team member's TEAM needs by using a total recognition and reward package. Although monetary incentives are usually limited in scope, non-monetary recognition is limited only by your creativity, awareness, and opportunities for recognition and reward on the job.

Part 2

How do I create and use a total RECOGNITION approach?

To create a total RECOGNITION approach we are offering you 3 tools. At the conclusion of the EXPECTATION setting stage(s), start your total RECOGNITION process. Start by first completing form (R) FLL: Recognition Menu for yourself. This form never gets shared with team members. The knowledge created on Form (R) is proprietary knowledge for manager use only. When you complete form (R) FLL: Recognition Menu, you must confirm your data and secure pre-approval by your Second Level Manager and the appropriate Human Resources Representative. Only then may you apply or use the knowledge gained from Form (R) with your team members. Remember at all times, the information compiled on the form remains confidential.

Team members receive the forms (R-1) Individual Recognition Interest Inventory and (R-2) TEAM Recognition Interest Inventory. It is important that both forms are handed out at the same time. Stress to each team member that the forms are confidential and voluntary to complete. If the team member chooses to answer any part of the forms he or she is then required to put his or her name on the forms. The greater the levels of trust within the TEAM, the greater the likelihood that the forms will be completed thoroughly. If you force a team member to complete any part of the forms, you will degrade team member trust.

If team members are reluctant to complete the forms, you may need to operate in the dark. However, as you perform your LEAD-ER duties notice which forms of RECOGNITION each team member welcomes or dislikes. Once team members see that RECOGNITION is part of their on-going work routine, they will start to trust the process and volunteer information about their true RECOGNITION needs. In order to make the total

Recognition

RECOGNITION approach part of team member(s) on-going work routine, utilize these forms during every EXPECTATION setting cycle, or bi-annually.

EXAMPLE

**Proprietary/Confidential
Management Document**

(R) FLL Recognition Menu

FLL name: _Preetha_   Date: _1/2013_

Complete this form bi-annually. ☑ Start/End year ☐ Mid year

MONETARY ELEMENTS — Identify relevant types or forms of monetary recognition.

Fixed		Variable		Benefits	
1.	base salary	2.	bonus	1.	medical
1.	wages	1.	commission	3.	flex time
		3.	spot awards	1.	tuition

NON-MONETARY ELEMENTS — Identify relevant types or forms of non-monetary recognition.

Work		FLL		Team members		Organization	
3.	Challenging	3.	Praise	3.	Celebration	2.	Food & Beverage
3.	Autonomy	3.	Delegating	3.	Peer acknowledgment	2.	Newsletters
3.	Work variety	3.	Coaching	3.	Peer coaching	1.	Parking perks

ENVIRONMENTS — Places where RECOGNITION can occur.

Work		FLL		Team members		Organization	
3.	On the floor	3.	FLL Office	3.	Staff meeting	2.	Annual meeting
3.	Break room	3.	On the floor	3.	Email	1.	Newsletter
3.	Parking lot	2.	Boss's office	3.	Peer coaching	1.	Anniversary dinner

DECISION MAKERS — Identify decision makers who can approve RECOGNITION options.

1.	Sarah	2.	Sarah	3.	Preetha
	Human Resources Director		Second Level Manager		First Line Leader

EXAMPLE (R-1) Individual Recognition Interest Inventory

Team member name: _Ed_   Date: _7/2012_

Complete this form bi-annually.   ☑ Start/End year   ☐ Mid year

This form is voluntary. The information you provide will help better create recognition tailored to you. Everything on this form is optional and confidential. Please hand this form back to your immediate manager for private discussion and review.

1. Prioritize and explain your *personal values (E.g. High integrity and morals)*:

1. Integrity: Ethics are very important to me.
2. Recognition/status: It's important how others see me.
3. Autonomy: I like freedom and independence.
5. Active lifestyle: I love playing and watching sports.
4. Learning: I am life long learner.

2. Prioritize and explain your *work values* (E.g. Perfection in all I do):

1. Perfectionist: I believe everything must be done right. 100% all the time.
2. Recognition/status: I want others to respect me and my position.
3. Autonomy: I want more responsibility, less supervision. No micro managing.
4. Development: I want coaching, feedback, and training to improve.

3. Prioritize types of recognition that you DO NOT value? (E.g. No gimmick awards.)

1. I don't like getting praise one-on-one only.
2. I don't need gimmick gifts. Ie. hats, cups, golf umbrella.
3. I don't like team awards that include slackers or non-performers.

4. Prioritize types of recognition that you DO value? (E.g. Genuine praise from my boss.)

1. Salary.
2. Travel allowance.
3. Title or visibility of position.
4. Praise from immediate boss and senior management.
5. Tickets to football games at company stadium box.
6. Lunches with boss and upper management.
7. Early time off on Friday's.

EXAMPLE

(R-2) TEAM Recognition Interest Inventory

Name: _Ed_   Date: _7/2012_

Complete this form bi-annually.   ☑ Half year   ☐ End year

This form is voluntary. The information you provide will help better create recognition tailored to you. Everything on this form is optional and confidential. Please hand this form back to your immediate manager for private discussion and review.

Prioritize types of recognition for the TEAM that you DO NOT value?

1. TEAM awards that reward slackers.
2. TEAM awards happen too infrequently. With too long intervals.
3. TEAM participation certificates that are meaningless.
4. TEAM dinners where we don't get to order/drink alcohol.

Prioritize types of recognition for the TEAM that you DO value?

1. Monetary.
2. Time off for meeting targets.
3. Company wide honors or recognition.
4. Monthly recognition of TEAM achievements.
5. Team dinners or events where plus ones are invited.

Part 3

A Culture of RECOGNITION

Culture is a way of life, and culture is unavoidable. The winds of the world are many, varied, and sometimes opportunistic and tempting. Neglect your TEAM culture and the winds will blow away parts of your TEAM. Shape your culture and you can brace against or use the wind to your TEAM's benefit.

The sleeping giant may be aware of the winds of temptation; only the sleeping giant sees those winds as the winds of interference because temptation lures away his or her best people. Sleeping giants react too late to tempted team members. They throw only money at the team member with the hope of inducing the team member to stay. This thinking is a form of insanity, because the sleeping giant is repeating the same RECOGNITION action but expecting different ENGAGEMENT and retention results. More money alone is rarely correlated to greater job satisfaction. So the madness persists for the sleeping giant because money is no match against a wind of temptation with an enticing whisper.

The LEAD-ER giant is constantly aware of the winds of temptation; only the LEAD-ER giant sees those winds as the winds of opportunity. Any new wind of opportunity is evaluated and considered for incorporation within the TEAM's total RECOGNITION and reward culture. If the wind carries something valuable, LEARNING occurs. When LEAD-ER giants are so attentive to the world around them, team members know that they won't find a better TEAM to join. There is no desire from the team member to seek fulfillment elsewhere, which is why winds of temptation won't adversely affect LEAD-ER TEAMS. LEAD-ER giants are the shapers of their culture of ENGAGEMENT and RECOGNITION.

Appendix: Giant Tools

Learning

(L-1) FLL: Personal Action Plan for SELF

Name: _____ Date: _____

Rank your preferred learning styles from best (1) to worst (3)?

☐ Auditory ☐ Kinesthetic ☐ Visual

Identify 3 action areas that support LEARNING about SELF. Model your 3 answers to match our example below.

Learning Area(s) to work on	Key action step(s)	Specific timeline(s)	Key resource(s)	Desired outcome(s)
Gain feedback about strengths and weaknesses as a leader to build and improve on.	STEP 1: Create annonymous system, administrator collects data.	ST 1: 1 week.	Boss, self, & administrator	Strengths protected, weaknesses addressed.
	STEP 2: Analyze data	ST 2: 1 week.	Self	
	STEP 3: Share with TEAM	ST 3: 1 week.	Self & TEAM	Behavioral
	STEP 4: Change behavior(s)	ST 4: x weeks.	Self & TEAM	changes.

Learning Area(s) to work on	Key action step(s)	Specific timeline(s)	Key resource(s)	Desired outcome(s)

Learning Area(s) to work on	Key action step(s)	Specific timeline(s)	Key resource(s)	Desired outcome(s)

Learning Area(s) to work on	Key action step(s)	Specific timeline(s)	Key resource(s)	Desired outcome(s)

LEARNING

Please thoroughly reflect on each question before writing your answers. Complete this form in private. Be prepared to discuss your answers with your team leader.

Team member name: _____

Position: _____

Date: _____

Key job duties: (List your five main duties only.)
E.g. In-store customer service.

1. _____
2. _____
3. _____
4. _____
5. _____

What do you think is the key knowledge required for each duty:
E.g. In-store customer service - product knowledge.

1. _____
2. _____
3. _____
4. _____
5. _____

What is the key skill or ability requirement for each duty:
E.g. In-store customer service - sales skills.

1. _____
2. _____
3. _____
4. _____
5. _____

What key knowledge and/or skills do I need to improve?
E.g. Closing the sale better.

1. _____
2. _____
3. _____

Can you identify any major learning obstacles you may have?
E.g. I get distracted by noise which hinders my listening.

1. _____
2. _____
3. _____

Expectation Setting

FLL name: _____ Date: _____

3 *Key Responsibility Areas (KRA)* for leadership of SELF.

WORK PLANNING: of team KRA, objectives, and essential behaviors.

PEOPLE PLANNING: of individual team member KRA, objectives, and essential behaviors.

TEAMWORK (CULTURE) PLANNING: Team/individual behavioral norms.

Objective Setting Stage   ☐ 3 months   ☐ 6 months   ☐ 12 months

Work Planning Objective

Team KRA are identified, communicated, implemented, and monitored for ongoing progress.

People Planning Objective

Individual KRA are identified, communicated, implemented, and monitored for ongoing progress.

Teamwork (Culture) Planning Objective

TEAM/Individual behavioral norms are identified, communicated, practiced, and monitored for ongoing progress.

Essential behaviors supporting KRA / Objectives

Behaviors: WORK PLANNING

_____
_____
_____
_____
_____

Behaviors: PEOPLE PLANNING

_____
_____
_____
_____
_____

Behaviors: TEAMWORK (CULTURE) PLANNING

_____
_____
_____
_____
_____

Expectation Setting

(ES-2) Alignment of TEAM responsibilities

FLL name: _____

Date: _____

FLL: Step 1

FLL lists all key responsibility areas (KRA) for the TEAM.

1. _____
   _____
2. _____
   _____
3. _____
   _____
4. _____
   _____
5. _____
   _____

FLL: Step 2

FLL identifies which team members are responsible for appropriate support in each KRA.

KRA	FLL	Team member name	Team member name	Team member name	Team member name	Team member name	Team member name
1.	✓						
2.	✓						
3.	✓						
4.	✓						
5.	✓						

FLL: Step 3

Analyze data for overserviced and underserviced KRA. Reassign responsibilities as needed.

FLL & Team: Step 1

FLL shares this preliminary document with the TEAM to confirm that all KRA have been identified, and that responsibility has been appropriately assigned.

FLL & Team member: Step 2

The FLL then has a one-on-one meeting with each team member to complete Form (ES-3) Assessment with TEAM MEMBER, and team member signs off on responsibilities.

E xpectation Setting

Team member name: _____

First Line Leader name: _____

Date: _____

3 key responsibility areas (KRA).

i. _____
ii. _____
iii. _____

List each job **objective** for each KRA. ☐ 3 months ☐ 6 months ☐ 12 months

_____
_____
_____
_____
_____
_____

Identify the key **behavior(s)** team member will demonstrate to accomplish each objective.

_____
_____
_____
_____
_____
_____
_____
_____
_____
_____
_____

Team member signature: _____

First Line Leader signature: _____

A ction

Name: _____ Year: _____

☐ Jan ☐ Feb ☐ March ☐ April ☐ May ☐ June ☐ July ☐ Aug ☐ Sept ☐ Oct ☐ Nov ☐ Dec

1. Walking-the-talk

How frequently am I walking-the-talk?

○ Never ○ Sometimes ○ Often ○ Always

Behaviors I like:
_____
_____
_____
_____

How effectively am I walking-the-talk?

○ Poor ○ Fair ○ Good ○ Excellent

Behaviors to improve on:
_____
_____
_____
_____

2. Sense of urgency

How frequently do I apply a sense of urgency?

○ Never ○ Sometimes ○ Often ○ Always

Behaviors I like:
_____
_____
_____
_____

How effectively am I applying a sense of urgency?

○ Poor ○ Fair ○ Good ○ Excellent

Behaviors to improve on:
_____
_____
_____
_____

3. Can-do attitude

How frequently do I apply a can-do attitude?

○ Never ○ Sometimes ○ Often ○ Always

Behaviors I like:
_____
_____
_____
_____

How effectively am I applying a can-do attitude?

○ Poor ○ Fair ○ Good ○ Excellent

Behaviors to improve on:
_____
_____
_____
_____

4. Reflection

How frequently do I reflect on ACTION?

○ Never ○ Sometimes ○ Often ○ Always

Behaviors I like:
_____
_____
_____
_____

How effectively do I reflect on ACTION?

○ Poor ○ Fair ○ Good ○ Excellent

Behaviors to improve on:
_____
_____
_____
_____

Development

FLL name: _____   Date: _____

Feedback relative to knowledge, skills, and abilities in my current position.

Please provide me with your input concerning how you view my personal strengths and weaknesses relative to my job knowledge, skills, and abilities. Please remain anonymous, but leave detailed feedback. If you could note at least 3 strengths and 3 weaknesses with examples for each, I'd be very appreciative. Thank you in advance. When you have completed this form please send it to: _____

_____

_____

For each section there is a feedback example to help guide your responses.

Strengths with explanation or example(s):

Eg. Great enthusiasm - everytime she enters the classroom she's smiling and animated. It's very stimulating and inspiring.

_____

_____

_____

_____

_____

_____

_____

_____

Weaknesses with explanation or example(s):

Eg. Lacks experience - It's clear that she's still figuring out how she needs to teach. She keeps changing how she teaches because she keeps seeing better ways to do things, but it's frustrating because there is no rhythm or flow to what she's doing.

_____

_____

_____

_____

_____

_____

_____

_____

Development

(D-2) Individual Development Plan

Name: _____ Date: _____

Summary of key strengths and key developmental improvement opportunities

STRENGTHS:
- _____
- _____
- _____
- _____

DEVELOPMENTAL OPPORTUNITIES:
- _____
- _____
- _____
- _____

Strength to leverage: (Be specific)	Development Plans/ Training Actions	Timeline/ Target Dates	Results

Strength to leverage: (Be specific)	Development Plans/ Training Actions	Timeline/ Target Dates	Results

Developmental opportunity 1: (Be specific)	Development Plans/ Training Actions	Timeline/ Target Dates	Results

Developmental opportunity 2: (Be specific)	Development Plans/ Training Actions	Timeline/ Target Dates	Results

Future positions, assignments, projects, and committees of interest:

_____
_____
_____
_____

Engagement

(Eng-1A) Level of TEAM ENGAGEMENT

FLL Name: _____ Year: _____

Complete this form
bi-annually or quarterly.
☐ Half ☐ 1st Q   ☐ End ☐ 3rd Q
☐ year ☐ 2nd Q   ☐ year ☐ 4th Q

Wholistically rate your TEAM on their current level of committment concerning each Guiding Principle. When rating, stress objectivity and realism in your assessment. Inflated scores make for a faulty tool.

Learning

Commitment Levels

Question	Lower (Awareness)	Low (Agreement)	High (Supportive)	Higher (Ownership)	Highest (Conviction)
Does the TEAM take responsibility for LEARNING?	1 ☐	2 ☐	3 ☐	4 ☐	5 ☐
How attentitive are my team members to their personal LEARNING style?	1 ☐	2 ☐	3 ☐	4 ☐	5 ☐
What is my TEAM's level of continuous LEARNING?	1 ☐	2 ☐	3 ☐	4 ☐	5 ☐
Do my team members LEARN from each other?	1 ☐	2 ☐	3 ☐	4 ☐	5 ☐
Do team members use their work environment to aid their LEARNING?	1 ☐	2 ☐	3 ☐	4 ☐	5 ☐

Expectations

Commitment Levels

Question	Lower (Awareness)	Low (Agreement)	High (Supportive)	Higher (Ownership)	Highest (Conviction)
Do team members consistently set high standards for performance?	1 ☐	2 ☐	3 ☐	4 ☐	5 ☐
How clearly, positively, and realistically do team members communicate?	1 ☐	2 ☐	3 ☐	4 ☐	5 ☐
Do team members use two-way communication?	1 ☐	2 ☐	3 ☐	4 ☐	5 ☐
What is your TEAM's level of expectation planning?	1 ☐	2 ☐	3 ☐	4 ☐	5 ☐
What is your TEAM's level of surprise avoidance and making assumptions?	1 ☐	2 ☐	3 ☐	4 ☐	5 ☐

Action

Commitment Levels

Question	Lower (Awareness)	Low (Agreement)	High (Supportive)	Higher (Ownership)	Highest (Conviction)
What is the TEAM's level of responsibility and accountability to achieve results?	1 ☐	2 ☐	3 ☐	4 ☐	5 ☐
What is the team members level of being visible, present, and accessible to the TEAM?	1 ☐	2 ☐	3 ☐	4 ☐	5 ☐
What is the TEAM's level of sense-of-urgency?	1 ☐	2 ☐	3 ☐	4 ☐	5 ☐
What is the TEAM's level of can-do attitude?	1 ☐	2 ☐	3 ☐	4 ☐	5 ☐
What is the TEAM's level of reflection on ACTION?	1 ☐	2 ☐	3 ☐	4 ☐	5 ☐

ngagement

FLL Name: _____ Year: _____

Complete this form
bi-annually or quarterly. ☐ Half ☐ 1st Q   ☐ End ☐ 3rd Q
                           year ☐ 2nd Q   year ☐ 4th Q

Wholistically rate your TEAM on their current level of committment concerning each Guiding Principle.
When rating, stress objectivity and realism in your assessment. Inflated scores make for a faulty tool.

Development

Commitment Levels

	Lower (Awareness)	Low (Agreement)	High (Supportive)	Higher (Ownership)	Highest (Conviction)
What level of ownership and accountability do team members take for their DEVELOPMENT?	1 ☐	2 ☐	3 ☐	4 ☐	5 ☐
How attentive are team members to their strengths and weaknesses?	1 ☐	2 ☐	3 ☐	4 ☐	5 ☐
Do team members perform ongoing DEVELOPMENT?	1 ☐	2 ☐	3 ☐	4 ☐	5 ☐
Do team members DEVELOPMENT within their work environment?	1 ☐	2 ☐	3 ☐	4 ☐	5 ☐
Do team members use multiple resources?	1 ☐	2 ☐	3 ☐	4 ☐	5 ☐

Total the points scored in each LEAD section. Each LEAD section has a maximum score of 25 points.

| Learning | ___ | Expectations | ___ | Action | ___ | Development | ___ |

• Identify your 2 weakest LEAD sections based on the total scores above.

[_____]   [_____]

• Then select and prioritize your weakest 4 to 6 specific TEAM ENGAGEMENT items from the 2 sections identified.

1. _____
2. _____
3. _____
4. _____
5. _____
6. _____

Now that you have identified your 4 to 6 high priority TEAM ENGAGEMENT items to improve on, next plan to meet with your TEAM to clarify and validate appropriate resources, processes, and behaviors as needed.

(Eng-2) The Commitment Spectrum Applied

Engagement

Using the Commitment Spectrum, think holistically about scoring each of your team members in terms of everything they do. Give each team member a rating at the end of every month - evaluate them on the same day for consistency. You should see trends developing that will inform your coaching and DEVELOPMENT in support of your team member. Then use the team member data to plot a TEAM trend. NOTE: All data should remain confidential and not be shared with team members.

J F M A M J J A S O N D

CONVICTION
· Exhilarated
OWNERSHIP
· Enthusiastic
SUPPORTIVE
· Eager
AGREEMENT
· Intrigued
AWARENESS
· Ambivalent

CONVICTION
· Exhilarated
OWNERSHIP
· Enthusiastic
SUPPORTIVE
· Eager
AGREEMENT
· Intrigued
AWARENESS
· Ambivalent

CONVICTION
· Exhilarated
OWNERSHIP
· Enthusiastic
SUPPORTIVE
· Eager
AGREEMENT
· Intrigued
AWARENESS
· Ambivalent

CONVICTION
· Exhilarated
OWNERSHIP
· Enthusiastic
SUPPORTIVE
· Eager
AGREEMENT
· Intrigued
AWARENESS
· Ambivalent

CONVICTION
· Exhilarated
OWNERSHIP
· Enthusiastic
SUPPORTIVE
· Eager
AGREEMENT
· Intrigued
AWARENESS
· Ambivalent

TEAM

CONVICTION
· Exhilarated
OWNERSHIP
· Enthusiastic
SUPPORTIVE
· Eager
AGREEMENT
· Intrigued
AWARENESS
· Ambivalent

Recognition

Proprietary/Confidential
Management Document

(R) FLL Recognition Menu

FLL name: _____ Date: _____

Complete this form bi-annually. ☐ Start/End year ☐ Mid year

MONETARY ELEMENTS Identify relevent types or forms of monetary recognition.

Fixed | Variable | Benefits

☐☐☐☐☐ ☐☐☐☐☐ ☐☐☐☐☐

NON-MONETARY ELEMENTS Identify relevent types or forms of non-monetary recognition.

Work | FLL | Team members | Organization

☐☐☐☐☐ ☐☐☐☐☐ ☐☐☐☐☐ ☐☐☐☐☐

ENVIRONMENTS Places where RECOGNITION can occur.

Work | FLL | Team members | Organization

☐☐☐☐☐ ☐☐☐☐☐ ☐☐☐☐☐ ☐☐☐☐☐

DECISION MAKERS Identify decision makers who can approve RECOGNITION options.

☐ ☐ ☐

Recognition

(R-1) Individual Recognition Interest Inventory

Team member name: _____ Date: _____

Complete this form bi-annually. ☐ Start/End year ☐ Mid year

This form is voluntary. The information you provide will help better create recognition tailored to you. Everything on this form is optional and confidential. Please hand this form back to your immediate manager for private discussion and review.

1. Prioritize and explain your *personal values (E.g. High integrity and morals)*:

_____
_____
_____
_____
_____
_____
_____
_____

2. Prioritize and explain your *work values* (E.g. Perfection in all I do):

_____
_____
_____
_____
_____
_____
_____
_____

3. Prioritize types of recognition that you DO NOT value? (E.g. No gimmick awards.)

_____
_____
_____
_____
_____
_____

4. Prioritize types of recognition that you DO value? (E.g. Genuine praise from my boss.)

_____
_____
_____
_____
_____
_____

Recognition

Name: _____ Date: _____

Complete this
form bi-annually. ☐ Half
year ☐ End
year

This form is voluntary. The information you provide will help better create recognition tailored to you. Everything on this form is optional and confidential. Please hand this form back to your immediate manager for private discussion and review.

Prioritize types of recognition for the TEAM that you DO NOT value?

_____
_____
_____
_____
_____
_____
_____

Prioritize types of recognition for the TEAM that you DO value?

_____
_____
_____
_____
_____
_____
_____

Glossary

Management Levels

Most organizations have 3 levels of management: Top Management, Middle Management, and First-Line Management. We recognize that organizations may use various factors to classify management positions within the 3 levels based on factors including: salary grade levels, position titles, or the actual work duties performed by each management position. Many organizations use all 3 factors in slotting management and supervisory positions into the most appropriate levels. We also recognize that smaller organizations may consolidate the 3 management levels into 2 levels – by overlapping the management duties performed by the traditional 3 levels.

Top Management

Often referred to as the Executive and Senior-level of Management within an organization.

Typical titles

CEO, President, Chief Operating Officer, Chief Financial Officer, General Counsel, General Manager, Vice President, Director, Division Head, Dean, Superintendent, Principal, General Officer, and Senior Manager.

General work duties performed

- Formulate and communicate organizational mission, vision, and strategic goals and objectives.
- Ensure long-term decisions about the overall direction of the organization.
- Ensure strategic planning with focus on objectives for the organization as a whole.
- Establish general policies to guide the organization.

Glossary

Typical role outcomes

- Sets agenda and ensures progress toward achievement of priorities across the organization.
- Organizational competitive position is maintained and improved.
- Measurement systems within the organization are aligned and ensure achievement of organizational results.

Middle Management

Often referred to as the middle level of management in an organization between Top Management and First-Line Management.

Typical titles

Middle Manager, Plant Manager, Functional Manager, Product-line Manager, Department Manager, Assistant Dean, Assistant Principal, Colonel, and Major.

General work duties performed

- Implement the objectives, plans, and policies of Top Management.
- Develop budgets, allocate resources, and monitor performance of related areas.
- Ensure tactical planning with focus on the actions needed to achieve strategic goals and objectives.
- Supervise, direct, and coordinate the actions of First-Line Management.

Typical role outcomes

- Strategic direction is made operational for the organization, business, or function.
- Cross-functional communication, coordination, and collaboration are ensured.
- Work unit or team goals are set and achieved; and teams are established to address organizational needs and priorities.

First Line Management

Often referred to collectively as First Line Leaders within an organization, and colle vely residing at the bottom of the managerial stratum. Often referred to as the *backbone   an organization that makes things happen.*

Typical titles

Front-Line Manager, Supervisor, Department Head, Foreman, Section Leader, Group Lead Team Leader, Project Leader, Lieutenant, Sergeant, Squad Leader, Teacher/Educato Coordinator, and Senior Professional.

General work duties performed

- Implement the plans of Middle Management and Top Management.

- Ensure operational planning with focus on short-term issues and priorities in support of implementing tactical goals.

- Ensure short-term operating decisions that directly impact and guide the performance of team members.

- Provide direction or coaching to non-supervisory personnel and typically provide performance assessment and recognition of team members.

Typical role outcomes

- Customers and end users show increased satisfaction with organizational products, services, and/or knowledge provided.

- High priority initiatives are planned for, implemented, and achieved.

- Work unit or team successfully incorporates organizational change into daily operational procedures.

About The Authors

Tony Barth

Tony has a BA degree in Psychology and an MBA degree – both from The Pennsylvania State University, with additional post-graduate studies gained from Syracuse University in Organizational Behavior.

During the mid 1980's Tony was a *co-architect* who helped to develop a High Performing Organizational (HPO) network – involving several prominent organizations from chemical manufacturing and process industries – for the purpose of studying and applying advanced leadership and organizational concepts, along with the exchange of best practices in support of high performing leadership organizations.

Tony has enjoyed a long, successful career as a senior human resource manager employed at the site, division, group, and corporate levels with several prominent international and domestic based organizations. In addition, he has extensive experience as a leadership and management workplace educator. He also enjoys a strong facilitation and Master Trainer reputation in international and domestic organizational settings.

When Tony is not busy teaching Business and Human Resources at various local colleges, he consults for his private clients through Barth Associates, a human resources and organizational effectiveness company.

Wiaan de Beer

Wiaan has a BA degree in Psychology and an Honors degree in Performance Studies from South Africa. He is about to finish his Masters in Teaching, Writing, and Criticism – from West Chester University in the United States.

As a First Line Leader and senior manager, Wiaan has worked in fields as diverse as film, theater, recreation, education, and human resources. More specifically Wiaan has written, directed, and coordinated numerous projects spanning Industrial Education, Film and Theater Productions, and E-Learning platforms for corporate entities.

Education fulfills Wiaan's greatest passion. He teaches Language Arts at a middle school, and Communications at a local community college.

Key Word Index